Norbert M. Samuelson

Library of Contemporary Jewish Philosophers

Editor-in-Chief
Hava Tirosh-Samuelson, *Arizona State University*

Editor
Aaron W. Hughes, *University of Rochester*

VOLUME 15

The titles published in this series are listed at brill.com/lcjp

Norbert M. Samuelson

Reasoned Faith

Edited by

Hava Tirosh-Samuelson and Aaron W. Hughes

BRILL

LEIDEN • BOSTON
2015

Cover Illustration: Courtesy of Arizona State University

The series *The Library of Contemporary Jewish Philosophers* was generously supported by the Baron Foundation.

Library of Congress Cataloging-in-Publication Data

Norbert M. Samuelson : reasoned faith / edited by Hava Tirosh-Samuelson and Aaron W. Hughes.
 pages cm. — (Library of contemporary Jewish philosophers, ISSN 2213-6010 ; volume 15)
 Includes bibliographical references.
 ISBN 978-90-04-30569-4 (hardback : alk. paper) — ISBN 978-90-04-30570-0 (pbk. : alk. paper) — ISBN 978-90-04-30571-7 (e-book)
 1. Samuelson, Norbert Max, 1936– 2. Jewish philosophy. 3. Judaism and philosophy.
4. Rosenzweig, Franz, 1886–1929. I. Tirosh-Samuelson, Hava, 1950– editor.

B5800.N67 2015
181'.06—dc23

2015029106

This publication has been typeset in the multilingual "Brill" typeface. With over 5,100 characters covering Latin, IPA, Greek, and Cyrillic, this typeface is especially suitable for use in the humanities. For more information, please see www.brill.com/brill-typeface.

ISSN 2213-6010
ISBN 978-90-04-30570-0 (paperback)
ISBN 978-90-04-30571-7 (e-book)

This paperback is also published in hardback under ISBN 978-90-04-30569-4.

Copyright 2015 by Koninklijke Brill NV, Leiden, The Netherlands.
Koninklijke Brill NV incorporates the imprints Brill, Brill Hes & De Graaf, Brill Nijhoff, Brill Rodopi and Hotei Publishing.

All rights reserved. No part of this publication may be reproduced, translated, stored in a retrieval system, or transmitted in any form or by any means, electronic, mechanical, photocopying, recording or otherwise, without prior written permission from the publisher.

Authorization to photocopy items for internal or personal use is granted by Koninklijke Brill NV provided that the appropriate fees are paid directly to The Copyright Clearance Center, 222 Rosewood Drive, Suite 910, Danvers, MA 01923, USA.
Fees are subject to change.

This book is printed on acid-free paper.

CONTENTS

The Contributors	vii
Editors' Introduction to the Series	ix
Norbert M. Samuelson: An Intellectual Portrait *Jules Simon*	1
A Critique of Rosenzweig's Doctrine: Is It Jewish and Is It Believable? *Norbert M. Samuelson*	41
The God of the Theologians *Norbert M. Samuelson*	47
The Concept of 'Nichts' in Rosenzweig's "Star of Redemption" *Norbert M. Samuelson*	67
The Challenges of the Modern Sciences for Jewish Faith *Norbert M. Samuelson*	81
Interview with Norbert M. Samuelson *Hava Tirosh-Samuelson and Aaron W. Hughes*	97
Select Bibliography	147

THE CONTRIBUTORS

JULES SIMON (Ph.D., Temple University, 1994) is Professor of Philosophy in the Department of Philosophy and the Scientific Director for the Center for Science, Technology, Ethics, and Policy (CSTEP) at the University of Texas-El Paso. Simon teaches, lectures, and publishes in the areas of phenomenology, ethical theory, aesthetics, and Jewish philosophy with special attention to the political implications of existing and new emerging phenomena in science and technology. Among his publications are *Art and Responsibility: A Phenomenology of the Diverging Paths of Rosenzweig and Heidegger* (Bloomsbury, 2011) and two edited volumes focusing on ethics and genocide: *The Double Binds of Ethics after the Holocaust: Salvaging the Fragments* (Palgrave, 2009) and *History, Religion, and Meaning: American Reflections on the Holocaust and Israel* (Praeger, 2000). He is also the coeditor of *Thought and Social Engagement in the Mexican-American Philosophy of John H. Haddox: A Collection of Critical Appreciations* (Edwin Mellen Press, 2011). Simon's work on ethical theory and environmental ethics has garnered international reputation, and he has lectured and taught in India, Mexico, Spain, France, Germany, Israel, England, Wales, Canada, Norway, and Finland, in addition to teaching and speaking in several universities in the United States.

HAVA TIROSH-SAMUELSON (Ph.D., Hebrew University of Jerusalem, 1978) is Irving and Miriam Lowe Professor of Modern Judaism, the Director of Jewish Studies, and Professor of History at Arizona State University in Tempe, Arizona. Her research focuses on Jewish intellectual history, Judaism and ecology, science and religion, and feminist theory. In addition to numerous articles and book chapters in academic journals and edited volumes, she is the author of the award-winning *Between Worlds: The Life and Work of Rabbi David ben Judah Messer Leon* (SUNY Press, 1991) and the author of *Happiness in Premodern Judaism: Virtue, Knowledge, and Well-Being in Premodern Judaism* (Hebrew Union College Press, 2003). She is also the editor of *Judaism and Ecology: Created World and Revealed Word* (Harvard University Press, 2002); *Women and Gender in Jewish Philosophy* (Indiana University Press, 2004); *Judaism and the Phenomenon of Life: The Legacy of Hans Jonas* (Brill, 2008); *Building Better Humans? Refocusing the Debate on Transhumanism* (Peter Lang, 2011); *Hollywood's Chosen*

People: The Jewish Experience in American Cinema (Wayne State University Press, 2012); and *Jewish Philosophy for the Twenty-First Century: Personal Reflections* (Brill, 2014). Professor Tirosh-Samuelson is the recipient of several large grants that have funded interdisciplinary research on religion, science, and technology.

AARON W. HUGHES (Ph.D., Indiana University Bloomington, 2000) holds the Philip S. Bernstein Chair in Jewish Studies at the University of Rochester. Hughes was educated at the University of Alberta, the Hebrew University of Jerusalem, and Oxford University. He has taught at Miami University of Ohio, McMaster University, the Hebrew University of Jerusalem, the University of Calgary, and the University at Buffalo. He is the author of over fifty articles and ten books, and the editor of seven books. His book titles include *Abrahamic Religions: On the Uses and Abuses of History* (Oxford University Press, 2012); *Muslim Identities* (Columbia University Press, 2013); *The Study of Judaism: Identity, Authenticity, Scholarship* (SUNY, 2013); and *Rethinking Jewish Philosophy: Beyond Particularism and Universalism* (Oxford University Press, 2014). He is also the Editor-in-Chief of *Method and Theory in the Study of Religion*.

EDITORS' INTRODUCTION TO THE SERIES

It is customary to begin studies devoted to the topic of Jewish philosophy by defining what exactly this term, concept, or even discipline is. We tend not to speak of Jewish mathematics, Jewish physics, or Jewish sociology, so why refer to something as "Jewish philosophy"? Indeed, this is the great paradox of Jewish philosophy. On the one hand it presumably names something that has to do with thinking, on the other it implies some sort of national, ethnic, or religious identity of those who engage in such activity. Is not philosophy just philosophy, regardless of who philosophizes? Why the need to append various racial, national, or religious adjectives to it?[1]

Jewish philosophy is indeed rooted in a paradox since it refers to philosophical activity carried out by those who call themselves Jews. As philosophy, this activity makes claims of universal validity, but as an activity by a well-defined group of people it is inherently particularistic. The question "What is Jewish philosophy?" therefore is inescapable, although over the centuries Jewish philosophers have given very different answers to it. For some, Jewish philosophy represents the relentless quest for truth. Although this truth itself may not be particularized, for such individuals, the use of the adjective "Jewish"—as a way to get at this truth—most decidedly is.[2] The Bible, the Mishnah, the Talmud, and related Jewish texts and genres are seen to provide particular insights into the more universal claims provided by the universal and totalizing gaze of philosophy. The problem is that these texts are not philosophical *on the surface*; they must, on the contrary, be interpreted to bring their philosophical insights to light. Within this context exegesis risks becoming eisegesis. Yet others eschew the term "philosophy" and instead envisage themselves as working in a decidedly

---

[1] Alexander Altmann once remarked:
   It would be futile to attempt a presentation of Judaism as a philosophical system, or to speak of Jewish philosophy in the same sense as one speaks of American, English, French, or German philosophy. Judaism is a religion, and the truths it teaches are religious truths. They spring from the source of religious experience, not from pure reason.
See Alexander Altmann, "Judaism and World Philosophy," in *The Jews: Their History, Culture, and Religion*, ed. Louis Finkelstein (Philadelphia: Jewish Publication Society of America, 1949), vol. 2, 954.
[2] In this regard, see Norbert M. Samuelson, *Jewish Faith and Modern Science: On the Death and Rebirth of Jewish Philosophy* (New York: Rowman and Littlefield, 2008), e.g., 10–12.

Jewish key in order to articulate or clarify particular issues that have direct bearing on Jewish life and existence.[3] Between these two perspectives or orientations, there exist several other related approaches to the topic of Jewish philosophy, which can and have included ethics,[4] gender studies,[5] multiculturalism,[6] and postmodernism.[7]

Despite their differences in theory and method, what these approaches have in common is that they all represent the complex intersection of Judaism, variously defined, and a set of non-Jewish grids or lenses used to interpret this rich tradition. Framed somewhat differently, Jewish philosophy—whatever it is, however it is defined, or whether definition is even possible—represents the collision of particularistic demands and universal concerns. The *universal*, or that which is, in theory, open and accessible to all regardless of race, color, creed, or gender confronts the *particular*, or that which represents the sole concern of a specific group that, by nature or definition, is insular and specific-minded.

Because it is concerned with a particular people, the Jews, and how to frame their traditions in a universal and universalizing light that is believed to conform to the dictates of reason, Jewish philosophy can never be about pure thinking, if indeed there ever can be such a phenomenon. Rather Jewish philosophy—from antiquity to the present—always seems to have had and, for the most part continues to have, rather specific and perhaps

---

[3] See, e.g., Strauss's claim about Maimonides' *Guide of the Perplexed*, perhaps one of the most important and successful works of something called Jewish philosophy ever written. He claims that one "begins to understand the *Guide* once one sees that it is not a philosophic book—a book written by a philosopher for philosophers—but a Jewish book: a book written by a Jew for Jews." See Leo Strauss, "How to Begin to Study *The Guide of the Perplexed*," in *The Guide of the Perplexed*, trans. Shlomo Pines, 2 vols. (Chicago: University of Chicago Press, 1963), vol. 1, xiv.

Modern iterations of this may be found, for example, in J. David Bleich, *Bioethical Dilemmas: A Jewish Perspective*, 2 vols. (vol. 1, New York: Ktav, 1998; vol. 2, New York: Targum Press, 2006).

[4] See, e.g., David Novak, *Natural Law in Judaism* (Cambridge: Cambridge University Press, 1998); Elliot Dorff, *Love Your Neighbor and Yourself: A Jewish Approach to Modern Personal Ethics* (New York: Jewish Publication Society of America, 2006).

[5] E.g., the collection of essays in *Women and Gender in Jewish Philosophy*, ed. Hava Tirosh-Samuelson (Bloomington, IN: Indiana University Press, 2004).

[6] E.g., Jonathan Sacks, *The Dignity of Difference: How to Avoid a Clash of Civilizations* (London: Continuum, 2003); Jonathan Sacks, *To Heal a Fractured World: The Ethics of Responsibility* (New York: Schocken, 2007).

[7] E.g., Elliot R. Wolfson, *Language, Eros, Being: Kabbalistic Hermeneutics and Poetic Imagination* (New York: Fordham University Press, 2004); Elliot R. Wolfson, *Open Secret: Postmessianic Messianism and the Mystical Revision of Menahem Mendel Schneerson* (New York: Columbia University Press, 2009); Elliot R. Wolfson, *A Dream Interpreted within a Dream: Oneiropoiesis and the Prism of Imagination* (New York: Zone Books, 2011).

even practical concerns in mind. This *usually* translates into the notion that Judaism—at least the Judaism that Jewish philosophy seeks to articulate—is comprehensible to non-Jews and, framed in our contemporary context, that Judaism has a seat at the table, as it were, when it comes to pressing concerns in the realms of ethics and bioethics.

Jewish philosophy, as should already be apparent, is not a disinterested subject matter. It is, on the contrary, heavily invested in matters of Jewish peoplehood and in articulating its aims and objectives. Because of this interest in concrete issues (e.g., ethics, bioethics, medical ethics, feminism) Jewish philosophy—especially contemporary Jewish philosophy—is often constructive as opposed to being simply reflective. Because of this, it would seem to resemble what is customarily called "theology" more than it does philosophy. If philosophy represents the critical and systematic approach to ascertain the truth of a proposition based on rational argumentation, theology is the systematic and rational study of religion and the articulation of the nature of religious truths. The difference between theology and philosophy resides in their object of study. If the latter has "truth," however we may define this term, as its primary object of focus, the former is concerned with ascertaining religious dogma and belief. They would seem to be, in other words, mutually exclusive endeavors.

What we are accustomed to call "Jewish philosophy," then, is a paradox since it does not—indeed, cannot—engage in truth independent of religious claims. As such, it is unwilling to undo the major claims of Judaism (e.g., covenant, chosenness, revelation), even if it may occasionally redefine such claims.[8] So although medieval Jewish thinkers may well gravitate toward the systematic thought of Aristotle and his Arab interpreters and although modern Jewish thinkers may be attracted to the thought of Kant and Heidegger, the ideas of such non-Jewish thinkers are always applied to Jewish ideas and values. Indeed, if they were not, those who engaged in such activities would largely cease to be Jewish philosophers and would instead become just philosophers who just happened to be Jewish (e.g., Henri Bergson, Edmund Husserl, and Karl Popper).

Whether in its medieval or modern guise, Jewish philosophy has a tendency to be less philosophical simply for the sake of rational analysis and more constructive. Many of the volumes that appear in the Library of

---

[8] A good example of what we have in mind here is the thought of Maimonides. Although he might well redefine the notion of prophecy, he never rejects the concept. On Maimonides on prophecy, see Howard Kreisel, *Prophecy: The History of an Idea in Medieval Jewish Philosophy* (Dordrecht: Kluwer, 2001), 148–56.

Contemporary Jewish Philosophers will bear this out. The truths of Judaism are upheld, albeit in often new and original ways. Although Jewish philosophy may well use non-Jewish ideas to articulate its claims, it never produces a vision that ends in the wholesale abandonment of Judaism.[9] Even though critics of Jewish philosophy may well argue that philosophy introduces "foreign" wisdom into the heart of Judaism, those we call Jewish philosophers do not perceive themselves to be tainting Judaism, but perfecting it or teasing out its originary meaning.[10]

The result is that Jewish philosophy is an attempt to produce a particular type of Judaism—one that is in tune with certain principles of rationalism. This rationalism, from the vantage point of the nineteenth century and up to the present, is believed to show Judaism in its best light, as the synthesis or nexus between a Greek-inflected universalism and the particularism of the Jewish tradition.

What is the status of philosophy among Jews in the modern period? Since their emancipation in the nineteenth century, Jews have gradually integrated into Western society and culture, including the academy. Ever since the academic study of Judaism began in the 1820s in Germany, Jewish philosophy has grown to become a distinctive academic discourse practiced by philosophers who now often hold positions in non-Jewish institutions of higher learning. The professionalization of Jewish philosophy has not been unproblematic, and Jewish philosophy has had to (and still has to) justify its legitimacy and validity. And even when Jewish philosophy is taught in Jewish institutions (for example, rabbinic seminaries or universities in Israel), it has to defend itself against those Jews who regard philosophy as alien to Judaism, or minimally, as secondary in importance to the inherently Jewish disciplines such as jurisprudence or exegesis. Jewish philosophy, in other words, must still confront the charge that it is not authentically Jewish.

The institutional setting for the practice of Jewish philosophy has shaped Jewish philosophy as an academic discourse. But regardless of the setting,

---

[9] This despite the claims of Yitzhak Baer who believed that philosophy had a negative influence on medieval Spanish Jews that made them more likely to convert to Christianity. See Israel Jacob Yuval, "Yitzhak Baer and the Search for Authentic Judaism," in *The Jewish Past Revisited: Reflections on Modern Jewish Historians*, ed. David N. Myers and David B. Ruderman (New Haven, CT: Yale University Press, 1998), 77–87.

[10] Indeed, Jewish philosophers in the medieval period did not even see themselves as introducing foreign ideas into Judaism. Instead they saw philosophical activity as a reclamation of their birthright since the Jews originally developed philosophy before the Greeks and others stole it from them.

Jewish philosophy as an academic discourse is quite distinct from Jewish philosophy as constructive theology, even though the two may often be produced by the same person.

Despite the lack of unanimity about the scope and methodology of Jewish philosophy, the Library of Contemporary Jewish Philosophers insists that Jewish philosophy has thrived in the past half century in ways that will probably seem surprising to most readers. When asked who are the Jewish philosophers of the twentieth century, most would certainly mention the obvious: Franz Rosenzweig (d. 1929), Martin Buber (d. 1965), and Emmanuel Levinas (d. 1995). Some would also be able to name Abraham Joshua Heschel (d. 1972), Mordecai Kaplan (d. 1983), Joseph Soloveitchik (d. 1993), and Hans Jonas (d. 1993). There is no doubt that these thinkers have either reshaped the discourse of Western thought for Jews and non-Jews or have inspired profound rethinking of modern Judaism. However, it is misleading to identify contemporary Jewish philosophy solely with these names, all of whom are now deceased.

In recent years it has been customary for Jews to think that Jewish philosophy has lost its creative edge or that Jewish philosophy is somehow profoundly irrelevant to Jewish life. Several reasons have given rise to this perception, not the least of which is, ironically enough, the very success of Jewish Studies as an academic discipline. Especially after 1967, Jewish Studies has blossomed in secular universities especially in the North American Diaspora, and Jewish philosophers have expressed their ideas in academic venues that have remained largely inaccessible to the public at large. Moreover, the fact that Jewish philosophers have used technical language and a certain way of argumentation has made their thought increasingly incomprehensible and therefore irrelevant to the public at large. At the same time that the Jewish public has had little interest in professional philosophy, the practitioners of philosophy (especially in the Anglo American departments of philosophy) have denied the philosophical merits of Jewish philosophy as too religious or too particularistic and excluded it entirely. The result is that Jewish philosophy is now largely generated by scholars who teach in departments/programs of Jewish Studies, in departments of Religious Studies, or in Jewish denominational seminaries.[11]

---

[11] See the comments in Aaron W. Hughes and Elliot R. Wolfson, "Introduction: Charting an Alternative Course for the Study of Jewish Philosophy," in *New Directions in Jewish Philosophy*, ed. Aaron W. Hughes and Elliot R. Wolfson (Bloomington, IN: Indiana University Press, 2010), 1–16.

The purpose of the Library of Contemporary Jewish Philosophers is not only to dispel misperceptions about Jewish philosophy but also to help nudge the practice of Jewish philosophy out of the ethereal heights of academe to the more practical concerns of living Jewish communities. To the public at large this project documents the diversity, creativity, and richness of Jewish philosophical and intellectual activity during the second half of the twentieth century, and early twenty-first century, showing how Jewish thinkers have engaged new topics, themes, and methodologies and raised new philosophical questions. Indeed, Jewish philosophers have been intimately engaged in trying to understand and interpret the momentous changes of the twentieth century for Jews. These have included the Holocaust, the renewal of Jewish political sovereignty, secularism, postmodernism, feminism, and environmentalism. As a result, the Library of Contemporary Jewish Philosophers intentionally defines the scope of Jewish philosophy very broadly so as to engage and include theology, political theory, literary theory, intellectual history, ethics, and feminist theory, among other discourses. We believe that the overly stringent definition of "philosophy" has impoverished the practice of Jewish philosophy, obscuring the creativity and breadth of contemporary Jewish reflections. An accurate and forward looking view of Jewish philosophy must be inclusive.

To practitioners of Jewish philosophy this project claims that Jewish philosophical activity cannot and should not remain limited to professional academic pursuits. Rather, Jewish philosophy must be engaged in life as lived in the present by both Jews and non-Jews. Jews are no longer a people apart, instead they are part of the world and they live in this world through conversation with other civilizations and cultures. Jewish philosophy speaks to Jews and to non-Jews, encouraging them to reflect on problems and take a stand on a myriad of issues of grave importance. Jewish philosophy, in other words, is not only alive and well today, it is also of the utmost relevance to Jews and non-Jews.

The Library of Contemporary Jewish Philosophers is simultaneously a *documentary* and an *educational* project. As a documentary project, it intends to shape the legacy of outstanding thinkers for posterity, identifying their major philosophical ideas and making available their seminal essays, many of which are not easily accessible. A crucial aspect of this is the interview with the philosophers that functions, in many ways, as an oral history. The interview provides very personal comments by each philosopher as he or she reflects about a range of issues that have engaged them over the years. In this regard the Library of Contemporary Jewish Philosophers simultaneously records Jewish philosophical activity and demonstrates its creativity both as a constructive discourse as well as an academic field.

As an educational project, the Library of Contemporary Jewish Philosophers is intended to stimulate discussion, reflection, and debate about the meaning of Jewish existence at the dawn of the twenty-first century. The individual volumes and the entire set are intended to be used in a variety of educational settings: college-level courses, programs for adult Jewish learning, rabbinic training, and interreligious dialogues. By engaging or confronting the ideas of these philosophers, we hope that Jews and non-Jews alike will be encouraged to ponder the past, present, and future of Jewish philosophy, reflect on the challenges to and complexities of Jewish existence, and articulate Jewish philosophical responses to these challenges. We hope that, taken as individual volumes and as a collection, the Library of Contemporary Jewish Philosophers will inspire readers to ask philosophical, theological, ethical, and scientific questions that will enrich Jewish intellectual life for the remainder of the twenty-first century.

All of the volumes in the Library of Contemporary Jewish Philosophers have the same structure: an intellectual profile of the thinker, several seminal essays by the featured philosopher, an interview with him or her, and a select bibliography of 120 items, including books, articles, book chapters, and public addresses. As editors of the series we hope that the structure will encourage the reader to engage the volume through reflection, discussion, debate, and dialogue. As the love of wisdom, philosophy is inherently Jewish. Philosophy invites questions, cherishes debate and controversy, and ponders the meaning of life, especially Jewish life. We hope that the Library of Contemporary Jewish Philosophers will stimulate thinking and debate because it is our hope that the more Jews philosophize, the more they will make Judaism deeper, durable, and long-lasting. Finally, we invite readers to engage the thinkers featured in these volumes, to challenge and dispute them, so that Judaism will become ever stronger for future generations.

NORBERT M. SAMUELSON: AN INTELLECTUAL PORTRAIT

Jules Simon

Norbert M. Samuelson is a scholar of medieval and modern Jewish philosophy, a constructive theologian, and an early proponent of the dialogue of Judaism and science. Through his extensive writings and organizational activities, he has made an original and lasting contribution to contemporary Jewish philosophy and to the study of Jewish philosophy in American higher education. An ordained Reform rabbi, he began his career as a Hillel director, but left the rabbinate to become a professor of Jewish philosophy at a time when both Religious Studies and Jewish Studies were being established as new academic departments. Through his organizational activities at the American Academy of Religion and the Academy of Jewish Philosophy, he stimulated the interest in Jewish philosophy in the 1980s and its growing reception within the American academy. Throughout his academic career he consistently argued that Judaism must be informed by contemporary science in order to be believable. As a constructive theologian and philosopher of religion he has been at the forefront of the new dialogue between science and religion, a conversation in which Jews are still underrepresented. A trained analytic philosopher, Samuelson brought clarity and precision to his exposition of Jewish beliefs, while arguing against the overly simplistic tendencies of analytic philosophy. As he deepened his knowledge of contemporary science, he creatively rendered Jewish traditional beliefs—creation, revelation, and redemption—in light of scientific knowledge in physics, cosmology, and the cognitive sciences. For Samuelson, what it means to practice Jewish philosophy is that the study of science and the engagement with philosophy express the love of God through the use of reason.

Biography and Career

Norbert M. Samuelson was born in 1936 and his work spans the end of the twentieth and the beginning of the twenty-first centuries. There are few contemporary Jewish philosophers who have produced a body of work that reveals such depth and breadth of knowledge of Judaism, Jewish philosophy, Western philosophy, and the history of science and mathematics. The reasons for this are based on two interrelated factors. First, Samuelson has a very broad definition of Jewish philosophy and a passionate dedication to all forms of Jewish philosophical activity, from the Bible and rabbinic sources (which he treats philosophically), through medieval Jewish philosophy (which he calls "classical Jewish philosophy") to modern Jewish philosophers. Second, Samuelson's original work of constructive Jewish theology employs science in general, and modern science in particular, to explicate and critique traditional Jewish beliefs. The breadth, depth, and complexity of his ideas have made his contribution to Jewish philosophy distinctive and unique.

Samuelson was born to Russian-Jewish parents. His father's family came to America in the late 1890s and settled in Chicago whereas his mother's family settled in Winnipeg, Canada, in the 1920s, after failing to secure entry to America. His mother eventually found her way to Chicago drawn by inchoate dreams of life in the allegedly glamorous city of Chicago. There she met and married Samuelson's father, who delivered neither glamour nor romance but a steady income of a U.S. Postal Service man and a middle class life. Desiring to give their only son the best that America could offer, his parents moved to the mostly Irish neighborhood of Rogers Park, where Samuelson (along with other Jewish children) attended public school, forging a Jewish identity through the rough and tumble contact with Irish children.

A precocious boy who loved sports, Samuelson's craving for learning was satisfied not in the mediocre Chicago public school, but in the Sunday school of Temple Beth Emet—The Free Synagogue in Evanston, Illinois, which at the time was led by Rabbi David Polish (d. 1995). This prominent leader of Reform Judaism in America introduced the young Samuelson to Judaism as an intellectually sophisticated, morally concerned, and socially engaged way of being in the world, a vision that has characterized his career, academic writings, and public persona. The early years in the Reform synagogue (which included exciting summer camp experiences) produced the vision that informed Samuelson's Jewish identity: Jewishness is a fusion of religiosity and intellectuality, of passionate commitment to justice and devotion to the pursuit of truth, of art and creativity.

Samuelson came into maturity in 1950s America, whose values, concerns, and political struggles would both shape Samuelson's choices as much as it would serve as the target of criticism and rebellion. Like other Jews who greatly benefited from America's public higher education, Samuelson enrolled at the public university of his hometown, the University of Illinois-Chicago Circle, but after two years he transferred to Northwestern University, where he majored in philosophy. At Northwestern he was exposed to first-rate teachers in philosophy and other disciplines of the humanities and relished the knowledge that philosophy sought to impart: clear thinking about the meaning of life. The 1950s were the heydays of existentialism and phenomenology and Samuelson relished reading Jean-Paul Sartre and Albert Camus and meeting Martin Buber on his first tour of American colleges. In his undergraduate experience in Northwestern University, Samuelson retained the passion for the study of religion, philosophy, and literature and the awareness that understanding the human condition cannot be limited to debates about ordinary language.

After receiving his B.A. degree in philosophy in 1957 from Northwestern University, Samuelson did not go to graduate school to pursue a degree in philosophy, as could be expected, but rather enrolled in Hebrew Union College–Jewish Institute of Religion in Cincinnati, the rabbinic seminary of the Reform movement. The decision to pursue rabbinic ordination rather than a Ph.D. in philosophy reflected both a commitment to live a Jewish religious life as well as an understanding that rabbinic school could guarantee steady and secure employment. At the Hebrew Union College he had to master Hebrew language skills, which the Reform synagogue in Chicago did not impart, and he was exposed to the Jewish textual tradition, Jewish history, and Jewish philosophy in systematic manner. Since most of the courses did not pose too much of an intellectual challenge, he also had time to take courses in English literature and drama at the University of Cincinnati, located literally across the street from HUC, expressing his love of literature and the arts. At Hebrew Union College he earned first a bachelor's degree in Hebrew Letters in 1959 and then rabbinic ordination and a Master's of Hebrew Letters in 1962.

Of all the teachers at Hebrew Union College, two in particular would have lasting impact on Samuelson: Ellis Rivkin (d. 2010) imbued in him an astute historical sensibility that shaped his tendency to understand philosophy in its historical context, and Norman Golb, the medievalist and Orientalist of the University of Chicago, who was a professor at HUC, and who imparted to him the necessary textual skills to study medieval Jewish philosophy. At HUC, Samuelson's intellectual career was set in motion: the reading of Jewish texts with the tools of Western philosophy and with attention to the historical context.

Soon after his rabbinic ordination, Samuelson began to publish articles on medieval Jewish philosophy. His first article, "Ethics, Theology, and

Occam's Razor,"[1] demonstrated how he brought his knowledge of Western philosophy to bear on the interpretation of Jewish texts, and it was followed by two articles on Maimonides and Gersonides, two of the most outstanding medieval Jewish philosophers whose works framed Samuelson's intellectual concerns and religious orientation for the following decades. Ordained as a rabbi, Samuelson could then have a steady job, but instead of going to the congregational rabbinate, he chose to serve as a director of the Hillel Foundation at Indiana University, Bloomington. His experience as a rabbinical student taught him that although he performed rabbinic functions well, he did not really enjoy being a congregational rabbi. By contrast, as director of a Hillel Foundation on a university campus, he could further develop his interest in philosophy and find an outlet to his artistic creativity and impressive organizational skills. Indiana University was a perfect choice because of its outstanding Philosophy Department and its internationally renowned Music School. Indeed, as Hillel director at Indiana University he not only continued to earn a Ph.D. in philosophy (1970), he also produced many intellectual and artistic programs that made the Hillel Foundation on that campus an exciting hub for intellectual and artistic activities for faculty and students.

America in the 1960s was a society in the midst of social, political, and cultural upheavals with the civil rights movement, the women's liberation movement, and the anti–Vietnam War movement, all of which thrived on college campuses. As a Hillel director, Samuelson was a member of Clergy and Laity Concerned, an organization founded in 1965 by the National Council of Churches, which became known in 1967 when it sponsored the White House demonstration along with the Mobilization Committee to End the War in Vietnam. Working with Christian spiritual leaders, Samuelson organized draft deferment and public protests against the war in Vietnam and participated in civil rights marches in Selma, Alabama. For a Reform rabbi to be deeply involved in the civil rights movement and the peace movement was not unusual—many other Jewish progressive rabbis (the most famous of whom was Abraham Joshua Heschel) were involved in these twin forms of social action—but Samuelson was also aware that social protest could easily become violent and undermine society.

In 1967 another momentous event took place: the Six-Day War in which Israel remarkably won over its Arab neighbors, unleashing idealism and enthusiasm among American Jews. Samuelson and his family went to

---

[1] Norbert Samuelson, "Ethics, Theology and Occam Razor," *CCAR Journal* (April 1966): 28–40.

Israel on his Fulbright grant to study medieval Jewish philosophy at the Hebrew University under the supervision of Professor Shlomo Pines, who codirected his doctoral dissertation. There he began to apply his training in analytic philosophy at Indiana University with Milton Fisk and Reginald Allen to the interpretation of medieval Jewish philosophical texts, with a focus on Levi ben Gershom (known as Gersonides) (1288–1344), the philosopher-scientist, theologian, and biblical exegete. Even more than Moses Maimonides, Gersonides would provide the intellectual role model for Samuelson's own work in the early part of his career.

The year in Israel during the euphoric days after the Six-Day War was by no means simple. Samuelson's dream of making aliyah to live in a just and democratic Jewish State was deferred by the harsh reality of a young state still struggling to forge its cultural and public ethos and to sort out its Jewish identity. In a country where Reform Judaism only began to make headways, it was hard to be a liberal Jew, given the political power and public influence of Orthodoxy and the lack of interest in liberal Judaism among secular Israelis. The year in Israel also brought him closer to the reality of Jewish-Arab relations and to the Israeli-Palestinian conflict as experienced especially by Arabs in Jerusalem whom he met in 1967–1968 when they studied Hebrew at a municipal language school in Jerusalem. Although Palestinian resistance to Israeli occupation of the West Bank was just taking off at that time, Samuelson was already concerned about the potential negative impact of the occupation on the Jewish State. With his rabbinic penchant for justice and concern for human rights, he began to express criticism of Israel's treatment of Palestinians, which would later bring on him some criticism at home in the United States.[2]

When the year in Israel was over, Samuelson did not return to Indiana University but rather accepted the position of Hillel director at Princeton University, where he held the post from 1968 to 1973. At Princeton he continued to be involved in the antiwar movement, but with a newly minted Ph.D. from Indiana University, he began to focus his energy on the teaching of Jewish studies, which was being established in American universities during the 1970s. In addition to his position as Hillel director at Princeton, he was visiting lecturer in the Department of Philosophy at Brooklyn College (1969–1970) and visiting associate professor in the Hebraic Studies Department at Rutgers University (1969–1973). Jewish studies at the time developed along with and because of the establishment of religious

---

[2] Norbert M. Samuelson, "An Appeal for One Palestinian," *Sh'ma: A Journal of Jewish Responsibility* 22, no. 412 (April 1991): 93–94.

studies departments in American universities, both private and public. These developments facilitated Samuelson's successful academic career and his activities in two professional organizations: The American Academy of Religion and the Association for Jewish Studies. The successful fusion of Religious studies and Jewish studies shaped his academic career.

Samuelson's first full-time academic position as assistant professor was at the University of Virginia (1973–1975), from where he accepted a position as associate professor in religious studies at Temple University. There he became full professor in 1987 serving until 1998, when he became the Harold and Jean Grossman Chair of Jewish Studies at Arizona State University, a position he still holds. During his long association with Temple University, Samuelson was instrumental in revitalizing the academic study of Jewish philosophy. He founded the Academy of Jewish Philosophy and served as its chairman (1979–1988) and as its secretary-treasurer from 1988 to 2002. Under his leadership the Academy for Jewish Philosophy during the 1980s organized many conferences on Jewish philosophy, published edited volumes of original essays, and began fruitful collaborations with Christian philosophers and theologians on topics of shared interests.

Throughout his long and steady academic career, Samuelson taught as a visiting professor in several institutions, including the Department of Religious Studies at Lancaster University, England (1972), the Department of Religious Studies at the University of Pennsylvania (1984), the Theological Faculty of the University of Hamburg (1993, 1995), and Cambridge University, England (2012), where he has life membership in Clare Hall. Additionally he held fellowships and/or visiting professorships at the Oxford Centre for Postgraduate Hebrew Studies at Oxford (1987), the Chicago Center for Religion and Science at the Lutheran Seminary of the University of Chicago (1992), and the University of Leeds (2005). The last two institutions signified his growing interest in the dialogue of science and religion, bringing a distinctive Jewish voice to a Christian dominated discourse and urging fellow Jews to become more attentive to science as a path to knowledge of truth about the world that God created. He was a founding member of the International Society for Science and Religion, and member of the board of directors and academic board of the Metanexus Institute, a nonprofit organization that promoted the study of religion and science worldwide with funding from the Templeton Foundation. At Arizona State University, he promoted the dialogue of science and religion and Judaism and science through undergraduate and graduate courses, book publications, and participation in faculty seminars and conferences on the relations of religion and science.

What Is Jewish Philosophy and Why Does It Matter?

Samuelson has been at the forefront of the professionalization of Jewish philosophy and its growing reception in American academia. As a Hillel director and a professor of religious studies in American universities, Samuelson taught scores of Jewish and non-Jewish students, guiding them to think systematically and deeply about Jewish faith and practice. This work flourished at Temple University in particular where the Department of Religious Studies under the helm of Paul van Buren and Leonard Swidler cultivated Jewish-Christian dialogue and brought to Temple University theological students from Germany. That exposure to German students would also play a role in his intellectual development, aligning with his interest in the modern German-Jewish philosopher, Franz Rosenzweig (d. 1929). The experience of teaching students of all ages, diverse backgrounds, and different levels of exposures to Judaism also contributed to a didactic style of writing. Desiring to be understood by all, Samuelson developed a penchant for explicating complex philosophical ideas in a lucid narrative style, which at times can appear to be deceptively simplistic. Indeed, several of his books are written without the conventional scholarly apparatus of footnotes and with relatively little mention of other scholars who have written on a given topic under consideration. Their scholarship is cited at the end of the book or a given chapter as "further readings," but is rarely engaged, because such engagement takes away from presenting his own interpretation of the primary sources. Indeed, it is to the primary sources themselves (be they biblical, rabbinic, or philosophic) that Samuelson was obligated first and foremost and which he read most closely to tease out their meaning and significance. On the one hand, the close reading of selected texts is very useful for students who try to acquire access to the past texts but, on the other hand, such a method does not allow the student to get an overview of the material. To do so, the student has to read Samuelson's textbooks, where his own distinctive and often controversial view of Jewish philosophy is stated somewhat programmatically.

What is Jewish philosophy? Samuelson's answer is spelled out most usefully in his *Jewish Philosophy: An Historical Introduction*.[3] Therein Samuelson summarizes the ideas of leading Jewish thinkers including Saadia Gaon, Judah Halevi, Levi ben Gershom (Gersonides), Hasdai

---

[3] Norbert Samuelson, *Jewish Philosophy: An Historical Introduction* (London and New York: Continuum, 2003), 3; new ed., New York: Bloomsbury Academic, 2006.

Crescas, Baruch Spinoza, Hermann Cohen, Martin Buber, and Mordecai Kaplan. These thinkers are situated in their historical and cultural contexts and their contribution to the arc of Jewish philosophy is spelled out. The selected thinkers are "philosophers who thought about questions like all other philosophers," and Jewish philosophy (as opposed to "Jewish thought") is characterized as "based on logical reasoning, rooted in claims drawn from experience, that purports to make the authority for its claims more than mere opinion."[4] Samuelson insists that when one studies Jewish philosophy one is "not concerned solely with the conclusions of the philosophers but also with the reasons for the conclusions," so that "the study of philosophy is a study of ways of thinking no less and possibly more than it is a study of what was thought."[5] Since thinking is done by people who live in a particular time and place, all ways of thinking have a history and a location. Thus, to study Jewish philosophy is necessarily to study it historically, paying attention to a particular time, place, and sociocultural conditions. The purpose of the book is to offer "a very general map of Jewish philosophy," acknowledging that a map is never entirely accurate.[6]

Whether one endorses Samuelson's mapping of Jewish philosophy or not, it is important to understand his arguments about the nature, scope, and importance of Jewish philosophy. To Jewish readers, the book argues that Jewish philosophy is not an aberration within Judaism but rather the very heart and core of the Jewish religious tradition. To be a good Jew one must be philosophically informed, precisely as Maimonides has instructed Jews centuries ago, because the canonic sources of Judaism—Scriptures and rabbinic texts—are no less than "revealed philosophy." To understand the speculative claims of the canonic texts of Judaism one must possess philosophic knowledge. The opening chapters of Part I provide the data to support the claim that "the Hebrew Scriptures are a philosophy" and more specifically that "Scriptures are primarily a philosophy of history that orders within it all conceptual subjects."[7]

This approach to the Hebrew Scriptures, which has been recently endorsed by several scholars,[8] has far fetching ramifications: First, it means that Jews who define themselves religiously must be committed to the

---

[4] Ibid., 5.
[5] Ibid., 6.
[6] Ibid., 7.
[7] Ibid., 71.
[8] See Yoram Hazony, *The Philosophy of Hebrew Scriptures* (New York: Cambridge University Press, 2012). This book has been widely reviewed in Jewish and Christian press and has generated a vigorous debate.

study of philosophy, which is defined as "occupying the middle of an epistemic continuum between mere opinion ('thought') and relatively high probability claims ('science')."[9] If the canonic texts reveal truths, they must be accessed by means of human reason, the faculty that enables humans to pursue truth and make truth judgments. Thus understood, the pursuit of truth is mandated by Scriptures, making the engagement in philosophy an inherently Jewish religious activity. Second, since God is truth, there is no necessary conflict between "philosophy" (i.e., the love of wisdom) and "religion" (i.e., the love of God). Similarly, there is no necessary conflict between "philosophy" and "theology." In another publication Samuelson defines Jewish theology as "any study of who or what God is and what God does, where to 'study' means to think reflectively and critically about what the Hebrew Scriptures say as their words are interpreted in a 2,000-year tradition of reflection and textual commentaries by rabbis as well as how those conceptions were translated into forms of communal worship in rabbinic liturgies."[10] Thus understood, Jewish philosophy and Jewish theology are viewed as distinctive but mutually enriching inquiries. But third and most importantly, Samuelson's way of telling the story of Jewish philosophy makes an argument about its continuous growth and change over time by virtue of ongoing exegesis of sacred texts. The Jewish philosophical project is inherently exegetical or reconstructive as Jewish thinkers in each and every generation encounter the truth of the canonic texts anew. Such a developmental conception of Jewish philosophy is not only past oriented; it is also a powerful argument about the future: if Jewish philosophy ceases to reinterpret the canonic texts in light of what is known to be true from contemporary philosophy, Jewish philosophy will be consigned to death and oblivion. Samuelson would spell out how to reconstruct Jewish philosophy for the future in his most recent book, *Jewish Faith and Modern Science: On the Death and Rise of Jewish Philosophy*,[11] which will be discussed below. For now let us turn to the message that Samuelson seeks to convey to non-Jewish readers of the book, especially to the philosophers among them.

Samuelson argues that in Western society and culture Jewish philosophy should matter to everyone and not only to Jews. Since Jewish philosophy is

---

[9] Samuelson, *Jewish Philosophy*, 6.
[10] See Norbert M. Samuelson. "Theological Issues: Survey," in *Modern Judaism: An Oxford Guide*, ed. Nicholas de Lange and Miri Freud-Kandel (Oxford and New York: Oxford University Press, 2005), 267–77 (quote on p. 270).
[11] Norbert M. Samuelson, *Jewish Faith and Modern Science: On the Death and Rise of Jewish Philosophy* (Lanham, MD: Rowman and Littlefield, 2009).

a central intellectual strand within Western philosophy and culture, what it means to be a Western-educated person is that one must be informed of Jewish philosophy. Outstanding Jewish thinkers (e.g., Maimonides, Gersonides, Crescas, Spinoza, and Cohen) and Jewish translations, modes of scriptural interpretation, scientific discoveries and inventions, and philosophical argumentation have deeply shaped the history of Western philosophy. Thus, Jewish philosophy is not external to Western philosophy but is a central, essential, and indispensable voice within it. To be ignorant of Jewish philosophy is intellectually inexcusable, although this is precisely the case in many departments of philosophy today.

This view provocatively challenges departments of philosophy in American universities where philosophy is commonly taught with little or no attention to history because the logic of the ideas alone is under scrutiny. Although he too was trained in the Anglo-American analytic tradition, Samuelson argues that that analytic philosophy is distorted if it dismisses or ignores history and culture. Against the reigning academic conventions, Samuelson claims that "to ignore history and sociology of ideas and to focus only on the logic of the ideas themselves is to distort the ideas. Philosophy studied as the history and sociology of philosophy is better philosophy than philosophy studied simply as philosophy."[12] Understanding how philosophers came to hold certain ideas at a certain time and place is no less important than judging the truth value of their ideas, because ideas are always products of a given sociocultural context. The insistence on the significance of history in philosophy can be seen as Samuelson's Jewish critique of contemporary philosophy. Put differently, Jewish philosophy is presented as a corrective to the way philosophy is currently practiced, with a call to fuse history of philosophy, history of ideas, and history of religions with analytic philosophy.

Samuelson's retelling of the story of Jewish philosophy combines history of philosophy with the precision of analytic philosophy. He called on his Jewish cohorts to master analytic philosophy and apply it to the study of Jewish texts, biblical, rabbinic, and philosophic. The history of Jewish philosophy should not be merely descriptive; it must also interrogate the claims of the past texts for their truth value, as analytic philosophers are called to do. But precisely because the study of the Jewish philosophical past pertains to deep religious and existential questions, the retelling of the Jewish past cannot remain strictly academic, divorced from one's Jewish

---

[12] Samuelson, *Jewish Faith and Modern Science*, 5.

religious commitment and an entire range of moral, ethical, and political considerations. Since Jewish philosophy is so crucial to being Jewish, Samuelson cogently argues, Jewish philosophy must be front and center in Jewish education and public discourse.

As a Liberal Jew, Samuelson's life project has been to explicate the historical development of the Jewish faith in constant dialogue with the intellectually best of the surrounding cultures. For Samuelson that entailed to consistently raise the question: How should rational Jewish faith be interpreted today, where "rational" means a faith informed by Jewish tradition in the light of a contemporary intellectual history of Judaism? Consequently, Samuelson has always maintained that sociopolitical events, such as the Holocaust and the "creation of the third political state of the Jewish people"[13] are significant issues demanding the attention of contemporary Jewish philosophers. But far more relevant to understanding his particular contribution to the ongoing evolution of Jewish philosophy was Samuelson's conviction that the most salient issue has become the relation of the modern human sciences with religion, and that this relation should be the main concern of Jewish philosophy now and in the near future.

Samuelson repeatedly turned to contemporary physics for explanations and understandings of the ontological order, noting that the problem with modern science is that all contemporary physics leave us with a universe devoid of any purpose or moral value. This led him to inquire into the relationship of psychology and revelation which traditionally meant raising the question "Who had the greater prophet: Jews, Christians, or Muslims?" This question was then usually answered in the monotheistic traditions on the grounds of a mutually accepted criteria of human perfection, that is, the more perfectly human the prophet, the greater his epistemic reliability. Historically this meant that classical philosophers (Jewish included) turned to the natural philosophies of their day, be it Platonism and Aristotelianism, which assumed fixed, eternal substances but with the possibility of evolution from one species or substance to another.[14] For example, the species of "human" was distinctly ordered in a cosmic hierarchy where it was situated between angels and animals. Members of each species sought to become the most perfect instantiation of the respective species, and thus would qualify to move up to the next higher level upon transformative death. This notion of perfection is somewhat akin

---

[13] Samuelson, *Jewish Philosophy*, 324.
[14] Ibid., 327.

to Hinduism's reincarnation cycle, but it is also significantly different. In the case of prophets, their attainment of intellectual perfection and excellence enables them to function as "transitional" beings who occupied the "borders" between humans and angels, the standard of excellence being rational thinking.

As a rabbi and a public intellectual, Samuelson holds that these philosophical issues are not merely academic; rather, they pertain to ethics which specifies how we should conduct ourselves. He notes that, classically, speech and intelligence were considered marks of human distinctiveness, but the only "moral" goal or purpose of any species, from the perspective of the natural sciences, is to perpetuate the species. That then entails, at least in the case of humans, a differentiation in gender for the sake of propagation and efficiency—women bear children and thus raise families and men hunt and fight according to their greater physicality and aggressiveness. But today, given technological advances, such a moral differentiation based on biological differences no longer has the moral force it once had. Thus, Samuelson envisions an open future that leaves undetermined any predictions for the future except the task of determining "the rational grounds on which the survival and flourishing of the Jewish people is possible."[15] This task must take into account the nature of the future, which means taking into account the nature of redemption. This became, for Samuelson, the task of constructive Jewish theology.

Given that self-assigned task, it should be kept in mind that the origins of Samuelson's life as a Jewish philosopher began with theology and the empirical conditions of his life as a Jew, as he himself notes in many of his publications.[16] In *Jewish Faith and Modern Science* Samuelson reflects on the limited nature of his perspective as a human entity by listing a number of different perspectives through which he sees and understands everything, such as having been born and raised in Chicago, growing up with the after-effects of the Great Depression, and the economic optimism that followed the end of World War II. Of all the factors that determined his particular perspective, however, Samuelson noted that "none is more important than my identity as a Jew,"[17] and, even more particularly determinative

---

[15] Ibid., 332.
[16] See, for example, Norbert M. Samuelson, "Travels of a Jew in Germany," *Journal of Reform Judaism* (1979): 62–72; Norbert M. Samuelson, "Science, Religion and a Medieval Philosopher," *KEREM: Creative Explorations in Judaism* (Winter 1992–1993): 65–74; Norbert M. Samuelson, "Shabbat in Hamburg," *KEREM: Creative Exploration of Judaism* (Spring 1995): 71–99.
[17] Samuelson, *Jewish Faith and Modern Science*, 142.

than that general designation, was that fact that he was "an only child of immigrant Jews of eastern European origin in a Chicago neighborhood of children whose parents were immigrants either from Ireland or Germany."[18] These comments are as telling as is his confession that he was raised in the tradition of Reform Judaism and that the course of his life was such that he actively participated in a variety of Jewish denominations, including growing up with the Reform tradition and then serving as a Hillel director as a young adult. Such experiences forced him to deal with a wide array of different kinds of Jews and prepared him for the time that he taught at Reform and Reconstructionist seminaries as well as for his role as a faculty advisor to a Chabad center at Arizona State University. They also prepared him for his many years of research and writing in American secular universities in the context of Jewish Studies and Religious Studies. For Samuelson the teaching of Jewish philosophy is not an arid academic discourse but a lived experience in which the pursuit of truth shapes every aspect of Jewish life.

History of Jewish Philosophy

As noted above, a key conviction that constitutes the signature of Samuelson's work is the argument that Jewish philosophy is not an aberration in the history of Judaism. His view is informed by his observation of the historical fact "that Jewish civilization has always been subject to the dominant influence of foreign, empiric cultures [and that] there is no discernible pristine element in anything Jewish. In the case of Jewish philosophy, the external influences are overt. But they are no less present in the early works of Jewish law as well as in the Hebrew scriptures."[19] This results in his claim that in the final analysis of evaluating the worth of something, "what seems to be correct (i.e., true and/or good) ought to be accepted, irrespective of the sources of the claim and/or activity."[20] This claim sheds light on the way Samuelson reconstructs the Jewish philosophical past. He focuses only on those thinkers that he deemed to be philosophically and historically significant, namely, the "best" Jewish philosophers, whose texts and ideas he subjects to close analysis. Betraying a philosophical rather

---

[18] Ibid.
[19] Norbert M. Samuelson, *Judaism and the Doctrine of Creation* (Cambridge: Cambridge University Press, 1994), 78. This book will be discussed at some length below.
[20] Ibid.

than historical mind-set, this argument means that not all Jewish thinkers are worthy of detailed study; "minor" thinkers are forgotten for a good reason. Since Samuelson is seeking to present Judaism as a rationally believable religion, he focuses only on those philosophers who contribute to this project. In the medieval or "classical" period of Jewish philosophy that means focusing on Saadia Gaon, Maimonides, Gersonides, and Crescas, whose views are succinctly summarized in the survey of Jewish philosophy mentioned above. What makes these thinkers "classical" is the fact that they explicated the meaning of rabbinic texts with the tools of classical philosophy, especially Plato and Aristotle.

Classical Jewish Philosophy

In the beginning of his career during the late 1960s, Samuelson's audience was fellow Reform rabbis, whom he wanted to see more informed about philosophy of religion and about the differences between philosophy and theology. He published a good number of essays in the *CCAR Journal* and *Judaism*, urging his fellow rabbis to become philosophically adept.[21] But in the 1970s, as his academic career began to take off, he broadened the scope of his intended audience and began to publish in prestigious academic venues such as the *Harvard Theological Review*, the *Journal of the History of Philosophy*, and the *Journal of the American Academy of Religion*.[22] In so doing, he was signaling to non-Jewish readers of these journals that Jewish philosophy is intellectually deep and worth studying and that a dialogue between analytically informed philosophers, Jewish and Christian, is both possible and desirable.

The 1970s were indeed years of rich growth for Jewish-Christian dialogue in the context of post-Vatican II and the emergence of the academic study of religion. Samuelson published numerous essays in a wide variety of jour-

---

[21] Among these early essays are Norbert M. Samuelson, "A Therapy for Religious Definitions: Guides and Agnosticism in Reform Judaism," *CCAR Journal* (June 1967): 19–27; "On Proving God's Existence," *Judaism* (Winter 1967): 21–36; Norbert M. Samuelson, "Quest for Past and Future," *CCAR Journal* (April 1969): 39–47, 96; Norbert M. Samuelson, "Philosophic and Religious Authority in the Thought of Maimonides and Gersonides," *CCAR Journal* (October 1969): 31–43; Norbert M. Samuelson, "Revealed Morality and Modern Thought," *CCAR Journal* (June 1969): 18–30.

[22] These early publications include Norbert M. Samuelson, "That the God of the Philosophers Is Not the God of Abraham, Isaac, and Jacob," *Harvard Theological Review* (January 1972): 1–27; Norbert M. Samuelson, "Gersonides' Account of God's Knowledge of Particulars," *Journal of the History of Philosophy* (October 1972): 399–416; Norbert M. Samuelson, "Ibn Daud's Conception of Prophecy," *Journal of American Academy of Religion* 45, no. 3 (1977): 883–900.

nals ranging over a variety of topics in Jewish theology, Jewish-Christian dialogue, Judaism and politics, cultural issues related to Judaism, and on metaphysics and ethics. The broad spectrum of his publications indicates Samuelson's deepening understanding of the historical relevance of Jewish religious, cultural, and sociopolitical identity, his own included.

In his recent survey of Jewish philosophy mentioned above, Samuelson places Maimonides as the pivotal figure of classical Jewish philosophy, discussing Jewish philosophers "before" and "after" Maimonides and devoting several chapters to Maimonides, but Samuelson actually considered Gersonides to be technically a better and more important philosopher. After publishing several essays on Gersonides, Samuelson's revised doctoral dissertation was published as a full-length book under the title *Gersonides on God's Knowledge*.[23] The fact that it was published by a Catholic press signified the growing interest of medieval historians and philosophers in Jewish philosophy. By the late 1970s the academic study of medieval Jewish philosophy was becoming academic "main stream," and that trend would continue for the following decades. Samuelson's focus on Part III of the *Wars of the Lord* was no coincidence, since the question of God's knowledge goes to the heart of the attempt to reconcile Judaism and Aristotelianism. For Aristotle, God is a mind that thinks itself; an eternal thought engaged in the act of self-contemplation. Is the God of Abraham, Isaac, and Jacob identical with the God of Aristotle? After all, the God of rabbinic Judaism is a person that knows what transpires in the world He created and God interacts with His creatures. The key challenge to the fusion of Judaism and Aristotelianism lies in the question of whether God knows particulars and how is such knowledge possible. Samuelson's detailed explication of Gersonides' theory of divine knowledge cannot be rendered here, but his astute observation about Gersonides' use of Aristotelian logic should be noted. Samuelson was the first to explicate the significance of *pros hen* equivocation for Gersonides' religious philosophy.[24]

If Gersonides was the zenith of Jewish Aristotelianism in the fourteenth century, he was definitely not the first, since the introduction of Aristotelian philosophy into Judaism began already in the twelfth century with Abraham ibn Daud (d. 1167). Samuelson's second book-length study was devoted to Abraham ibn Daud's *Emunah Ramah*. The book included an English translation of the original Judeo-Arabic text into English and a

---

[23] Norbert M. Samuelson, *Gersonides on God's Knowledge* (Toronto: The Pontifical Institute, 1977).
[24] See ibid., 77–79.

thematic exposition of ibn Daud's rationalist reformulations of Judaism in Aristotelian categories. The systematic analysis of *Exalted Faith* provides a very useful and accessible exposition of Jewish Aristotelian philosophy, covering logic, physics, psychology, epistemology, metaphysics (that is, theology), ethics, and politics. To understand ibn Daud's fusion of Judaism and Aristotelianism, however, one had to turn not to Averroes (as was the case of Gersonides) but rather to Avicenna (d. 1037), the Muslim philosopher-physician.[25] Once again, Samuelson's pioneering work paved the way for other scholars to follow suit, thus contributing to scholarship on medieval Jewish philosophy.

By the 1980s programs in Jewish studies flourished in many American universities. Samuelson's scholarship and organizational work was crucial for making Jewish philosophy into an intellectually stimulating and Jewishly relevant discourse within Jewish studies. This was accomplished by the Academy for Jewish Philosophy, which Samuelson helped found and manage. The annual meetings of the academy not only generated the awareness that Jewish philosophy should receive due attention within Jewish Studies (alongside biblical studies, rabbinics, history, and literature) but also that Jewish philosophy merits philosophical attention. The activities of the Academy of Jewish Philosophy are showcased in a volume edited by Samuelson, *Studies in Jewish Philosophy: Collected Essays of the Academy for Jewish Philosophy, 1980–1985*.[26] A quick perusal of the Table of Contents captures the themes that concerned the Academy and that shaped the academic discourse of Jewish philosophy: Part I: "What Is Jewish Philosophy?"; Part II: "Reason Revelation as Authority in Judaism"; Part III: "Judaism and Language"; Part IV: "Judaism and the Philosophy of History"; Part V: "Modern Jewish Philosophy from the Perspective of Maimonides' Philosophy"; Part VI: "Modern Jewish Philosophy from the Perspective of Halakhah." These headings summarize how the contributors (including David Novak, Alfred Ivry, Menachem Kellner, Eugene Borowitz, Kenneth Seeskin, and J. David Bleich) defined and shaped the academic discourse on Jewish philosophy in the 1980s and 1990s.

What made the Academy for Jewish Philosophy distinctive and influential was the fact that it included Jews from across the religious spectrum of Judaism (e.g., Reform, Conservative, Reconstructionist, and Orthodox),

---

[25] The indebtedness of ibn Daud to Avicenna is explicated in detail in Amira Eran, *From Simple Faith to Sublime Faith* (Tel Aviv: Hakibbutz ha-Meuchad, 1998) (Hebrew).

[26] Norbert M. Samuelson, ed., *Studies in Jewish Philosophy: Collected Essays of the Academy for Jewish Philosophy, 1980–1985* (Lanham, MD: University Press of America, 1987).

that its members insisted on engaging the philosophic texts analytically and not just descriptively, and that participants insisted on the relevance of Jewish philosophy to contemporary Jewish life. Significantly, the Academy of Jewish Philosophy in the 1980s was a bastion of Jewish men, although a few women (especially in Israel and in France) were engaged in the study of medieval Jewish philosophy and a few (i.e., Sarah Heller-Willensky, Rivkah Horowitz, Rivkah Schatz-Uffenheimer, and Collette Sirat) were already established scholars. Systematic reflections on women and gender would begin to shape the discourse of Jewish philosophy only in the 1990s, even though Jewish feminism was already thriving since the 1970s.

Samuelson contributed several essays to the collection, all of which were previously published, each capturing where the discipline of Jewish philosophy was at the time.[27] The most original essay, "Judaism and History: A Mathematical Model for a Pluralistic Universe," presented a philosophical exposition of history which sheds light on the trajectory of his scholarship. Echoing the interest in philosophy of history he received from his teacher, Ellis Rivkin, Samuelson argues that

> the process of formulating an adequate conception of human history that presupposes a pluralistic universe in which God is one but only one determiner of events is vastly more complicated than the comparatively, simplistic, monistic model with which classical Jewish thought has operated. But what it lacks in simplicity it gains in rationality, i.e., after two thousand years of following a monistic model of interpreting the biblical conception of divine history in both human events and the cosmos, it is time to devote some effort to developing a pluralistic model which is closer to the literal meaning of the prophetic texts and at the same time is more likely to yield a verifiable ordering of history insofar as we know it.[28]

Since the paper is based on mathematics (a topic in which Samuelson gained more knowledge during the 1980s while teaching at Temple University), it is not accessible to most readers. However, that insight guided Samuelson's work in the following decades, explaining why he was attracted to process

---

[27] Norbert M. Samuelson, "Issues for Jewish Philosophy: Jewish Philosophy in the 1980s," in *Studies in Jewish Philosophy*, 43–59; Norbert M. Samuelson, "Possible and Preferred Relations between Reason and Revelation as Authority in Judaism," ibid., 127–42; Norbert M. Samuelson, "Reflections on the Logic of Inter-Religious Dialogue," ibid., 235–66; Norbert M. Samuelson, "Judaism and History: A Mathematical Model for a Pluralistic Universe," ibid., 267–88.

[28] Norbert M. Samuelson, "Judaism and History: A Mathematical Model for a Pluralistic Universe," in *Studies in Jewish Philosophy*, 285–86.

philosophy and why he found Franz Rosenzweig as the most intellectually compelling Jewish thinker.

Samuelson was among the first scholars to think about Jewish philosophy in terms of process philosophy.[29] The goal of process philosophy was to move away from the tendency of Western metaphysics to focus on *things* and instead to focus on processes and events, items better indicated by verbs than by nouns. Process philosophers focus on *becoming* rather than *being*, and they offer a new framework for metaphysics: time and change are principal categories of metaphysical understanding; processes are more fundamental than things; in the ontological repertoire major elements (i.e., God, Nature, persons, or substances) are understood as processes; and contingency, emergence, novelty, and creativity are fundamental categories of metaphysical analysis.[30] In his "Theodicy in Jewish Philosophy and David Griffin's Process Theology,"[31] Samuelson offered an original reading of the medieval thinker in light of the contemporary Christian process theology. Samuelson focused on Gersonides because Gersonides' writings "reflect Jewish philosophy at its most sophisticated, technical best in the classical period,"[32] but more perceptively the justification to single out Gersonides is that he gained a better command of Aristotle's natural philosophy, including biology. Hence, in the writings of Gersonides one finds attention to biology that was not common in other medieval Jewish philosophers, and it is this attention that provides the link between medieval philosophy and modern process philosophy, since biology is all about the process of growth and decay. Samuelson does not systematically explicate Gersonides' biology,[33] but he was one of the first scholars to pay attention to the philosophical and theological implications of Gersonides' interest in biology.

---

[29] There were other Jewish theologians, mostly progressive rabbis, who began to engage process philosophy in the 1990s. The most systematic example is William E. Kaufman, *The Evolving God in Jewish Process Theology* (New York: Mellen Press, 1997), which Samuelson reviewed in *CCAR Journal* (Summer 1998): 102–5. For a collection of essays that brought Jewish theology and process philosophy in conversation with each other, see Sandra B. Lubarsky and David Ray Griffin, eds., *Jewish Theology and Process Thought* (New York: SUNY Press, 1996). Samuelson's contribution to this volume is discussed below.

[30] This brief characterization of process philosophy is indebted to Nicholas Rescher, *Process Philosophy: A Survey of Basic Issues* (Pittsburgh: University of Pittsburgh Press, 2000).

[31] Norbert M. Samuelson, "Theodicy in Jewish Philosophy and David Griffin's Process Theology," in *Jewish Theology and Process Thought*, 127–42.

[32] Ibid., 127.

[33] Ahuvah Gaziel, "The Biology of Ralbag," Ph.D. Dissertation, Bar Ilan University (Ramat Gan, Israel) 2008 (Hebrew).

It was the interest in process philosophy that enabled Samuelson to bridge medieval and modern philosophy and begin to develop the project that does justice to Judaism as philosophy of history. The comparative reading of Gersonides and David Griffin bridges the classical and modern worlds of Jewish philosophy with the help of modern mathematics and science, indicating Samuelson's distinct style of philosophizing. Samuelson's desire at that time in his life to understand processes also indicates his growing fascination with and admiration for Franz Rosenzweig, who Samuelson considered to be the most important example of a Jewish process philosopher in the twentieth century. In Gersonides' philosophy, Samuelson found the fundamental mathematical principles of possibility and vector analysis that, in Samuelson's interpretation, was uniquely developed in modern Jewish philosophy by Rosenzweig.

From the late 1980s to the present, Samuelson's scholarship would increasingly focus on modern Jewish philosophy, explicating it for the general readers and for specialists. Due to his efforts, scholarship on Jewish philosophy grew in scope, depth, and appeal, gaining a place of honor within the non-Jewish academy and for the past three decades many academic presses established special book series on Jewish philosophy (both medieval and modern), signaling the greater respectability of Jewish philosophy in the Western academy.[34] All of this could not have happened without the work of Samuelson and other scholars of the Academy for Jewish Philosophy.

Modern Jewish Philosophy

Since the late 1980s Samuelson's scholarship has increasingly shifted from medieval to modern Jewish philosophy, offering a highly original interpretation of its key exponents. The interpretation is based on several interrelated commitments, beginning with his training in classical, medieval

---

[34] A few examples of this trend include Daniel H. Frank and Oliver Leaman, eds., *History of Jewish Philosophy* (New York and London: Routledge, 1997); Daniel Frank and Oliver Leaman, eds., *The Cambridge Companion of Medieval Jewish Philosophy* (Cambridge: Cambridge University Press, 2003); Steven Nadler and T. M. Rudavsky, eds., *The Cambridge History of Jewish Philosophy: From Antiquity through the Seventeenth Century* (Cambridge and New York: Cambridge University Press, 2009); Zachary Braiterman, Martin Kavka, and David Novak, eds., *The Cambridge History of Jewish Philosophy: The Modern Era* (Cambridge and New York: Cambridge University Press, 2012). To the first book, Samuelson contributed the chapter on Abraham ibn Daud; to the third book, Samuelson contributed the chapter on logic and language, and to the fourth book, he contributed a chapter on redemption.

Jewish philosophy as a basis for engaging in the best thinking that modern Jewish philosophy has produced, on the one hand, and a deep and a thoughtful engagement with modern science, on the other hand. This is consistent with his conviction that Judaism has always developed historically in relation to the sociopolitical and cultural conditions in which Jews found themselves. In saying that, Samuelson displays his orientation towards those Jewish thinkers who themselves attempted to live out their Jewish beliefs in the context of the more dominant cultures in which they found themselves. For Samuelson, this meant taking measure of the ways in which several of the most significant modern philosophers contributed to change the ways that Jews in modernity think about and act upon what is most important to their lives in understanding the formative influences that shaped their notions of identity, as Jews and as human beings. Of these, none is more important than Franz Rosenzweig, although Samuelson also pays attention to other seminal modern Jewish philosophers such as Baruch Spinoza, Moses Mendelssohn, Hermann Cohen, Martin Buber, Mordecai Kaplan, and Emil Fackenheim. Like its medieval antecedent, modern Jewish philosophy did not begin with any one of those philosophers and their unique ideas; rather, it began with an historical event that signified both continuity and a break with medieval Jewish philosophy and the emergence of new forms of normative rabbinic Judaism, which included also Kabbalah. Although Samuelson is not a student of Kabbalah, in his later works he refers to it as an integral part of Jewish philosophy, following the lead of Elliot Wolfson.[35]

In several textbooks designed for students and general readers, Samuelson offered highly readably expositions of modern Jewish philosophers. In his *An Introduction to Modern Jewish Philosophy* (1989),[36] Samuelson presents modern Jewish philosophy as an outcome of a traumatic historical event: the expulsion of the Jews from Spain in 1492. In this narrative, 1492 marks the beginning of modern Judaism because it shifted Jewish demography with consequent migration to the New World, to Western and Eastern Europe, and especially to Safed, Palestine. Historical changes shaped "the

---

[35] Elliot Wolfson, "Jewish Mysticism: A Philosophical Overview," in Frank and Leaman, *History of Jewish Philosophy*, 450–98.

[36] Norbert M. Samuelson, *An Introduction to Modern Jewish Philosophy* (Albany: SUNY Press, 1989). For his more recent overviews of modern Jewish philosophy, consult Norbert M. Samuelson, *Jewish Philosophy: An Historical Introduction*, 245–334. For a short exposition of "modern Jewish theology," see Norbert M. Samuelson, "Theological Issues: Survey," in de Lange and Freud-Kandel, *Modern Judaism: An Oxford Guide*, 267–77.

transition of the Jewish People into the modern world,"[37] posing new kinds of challenges to Jews, which are still with us today. This textbook too seeks to present the modern Jewish experience to students who know little about Jews and Judaism. The narrative discusses seminal historical events and trends (e.g., the emancipation, migration to America, modern anti-Semitism, the Holocaust, Zionism, and the founding of the State of Israel) and the diverse Jewish philosophical responses to these trends. At the end of each chapter there are review questions that enable students to grasp the emergence of secular and nonobservant forms of modern Judaism as well as the reformulation and reconstruction of traditional Judaism in the modern period. Characteristic of his exegetical style, Samuelson's in-depth sketches of individual thinkers does not study them to "defend their conclusions" but to be able to "make new thought moves and in solving new problems." For example, in his chapter on "Emil Fackenheim and Contemporary Jewish Philosophy" he begins by noting that, "religious philosophy necessarily is polemic. If there was no challenge to Judaism from the outside—if there was no system of thought outside of Judaism that was taken seriously—then there would be nothing to talk about in Jewish philosophy. It is the external challenge that determines the agenda."[38] These thoughts are the key to understanding the distinctiveness of Samuelson's approach, and this is the position that he consistently took throughout the development of his body of work.

Without a doubt, the key figure for Samuelson in the canon of modern Jewish philosophers is Franz Rosenzweig, who is perhaps the most unique and philosophically significant philosopher. Samuelson began his involvement with Rosenzweig's philosophy in the 1980s after learning about his philosophy in 1981 in a lecture on Rosenzweig and Buber given by Rivkah Horowitz in Philadelphia. Impressed by her account, Samuelson began a detailed and extended period of reading and annotating Rosenzweig's *The Star of Redemption* that resulted in a comprehensive commentary on the text, *A User's Guide to Franz Rosenzweig's The Star of Redemption*.[39] This book was developed over the course of twenty years of a weekly two-hour seminar session where small groups of graduate students would gather at Samuelson's home in Philadelphia to read the text with him, line by line, and paragraph by paragraph simultaneously consulting William Hallo's English

---

[37] Samuelson, *An Introduction to Modern Jewish Philosophy*, 26.
[38] Ibid., 288.
[39] Norbert M. Samuelson, *A User's Guide to Franz Rosenzweig's Star of Redemption* (Surrey, England: Curzon Press, 1999).

translation and Rosenzweig's original German text, along with countless sources from Samuelson's own library. In this way, the sessions took on the form of a Jewish *havurah* study group, the traditional form of Jewish mentoring education where a rabbi instructs a handful of select students over the course of many years in the textual traditions of Judaism. Working together, they provided clear prose interpretations of Rosenzweig's text in keeping with Samuelson's intent: "to present the *PASHAT* (simple meaning) of the text, and not *REMES* (what the text alludes to), *DeRASH* (how the text may be applied to contemporary situations), or *SOD* (what the text may mean at a deeper conceptual or spiritual level)."[40] Samuelson's close reading of the text is the most detailed "guide" to Rosenzweig's *magnum opus* but it is a demanding read, precisely because it is a linear commentary, following the age-old Jewish exegetical tradition. For general and more accessible summaries of Rosenzweig, one could consult Samuelson's textbooks, especially *Jewish Philosophy: An Historical Introduction*, chapters 27–29, where a succinct summary is offered. For the academic community of experts on Rosenzweig (which comprises Jews and non-Jews all over the world), Samuelson has written on various aspects of Rosenzweig's *Star of Redemption* and has presented papers in many international conferences and workshops.

Having become involved in the community of Rosenzweig scholars, Samuelson became ever-more convinced of the importance of Rosenzweig's philosophy, as quintessentially modern Jewish philosophy. In fact, he was instrumental in founding the International Rosenzweig Society (International Rosenzweig Gesellschaft; IRG) after inviting most of the intellectuals who were at that time doing significant work out of Rosenzweig's heritage to meet at Arizona State University in 2002, to discuss creating this academic society. Two years later the IRG was officially established in Kassel, Germany, and Samuelson was elected as Honorary President on the Board of the Society. Rosenzweig's ideas have permeated Samuelson's thoughts and published writings, and the insightfulness of his clear and distinct interpretations are unrivaled in the field of Rosenzweig studies. It is likely that Samuelson's enduring contribution to the heritage of a "living" Jewish philosophy rests upon the ways in which he took up and was influenced by Rosenzweig's writings.[41] In fact, Samuelson's read-

---

[40] Samuelson, *A User's Guide*, xxiii.
[41] The general scholarship on Rosenzweig is too numerous to be cited here, indicating his centrality for contemporary Jewish philosophy understood both as academic discourse and as constructive Jewish theology.

ing of Rosenzweig became the occasion that enabled him to fuse rabbinic Judaism, Jewish philosophy, science and mathematics, and process philosophy to create his own very distinctive constructive philosophy.

Why is Rosenzweig so important for contemporary Jewish philosophy and for Samuelson in particular? *A User's Guide* reveals to us several core insights about Samuelson's commitments as a Jewish philosopher. First and foremost, Samuelson is dedicated to learning from the best of Jewish philosophers and, for him, Rosenzweig is by far the best Jewish philosopher of the modern period. Rosenzweig was an expert in the best philosophies of his day, namely, Descartes, Spinoza, Kant, Hegel, Schelling, Kierkegaard, Nietzsche, and Hermann Cohen. Additionally, he was immersed in Goethe's poetic and aesthetic worldview and studied history with Friedrich Meinecke. Rosenzweig was deeply engaged in philosophy, literature, culture, politics, science, and religion of early twentieth-century Germany. Similarly, Samuelson's own work grew out of his deep engagement in the philosophy, literature, culture, politics, science, and religion of the later twentieth and early twenty-first centuries of the United States. Of course, there is a difference between Rosenzweig and Samuelson. Unlike Rosenzweig, whose primary interests were rooted in the cultural and practical aesthetics of his day, and which led to Rosenzweig distancing himself from direct involvement in the political and educational institutions of Weimar Germany, Samuelson decided to pursue the life of a Jewish philosopher within academia and committed himself to the ongoing engagement with the very best science and philosophy of his day. In effect, Samuelson chose his own path in Jewish philosophy and did so in such a way that, like Rosenzweig, his choices and his body of work will continue to inspire others who care about how Jewish philosophy can continue to contribute to the richness and progress of human wisdom.

There are many scholars today who write on modern Jewish philosophy by focusing on Rosenzweig, but very few also possess the knowledge of medieval Jewish philosophy. Since Samuelson came to the study of Rosenzweig after he developed his expertise in classical Jewish philosophy, it is not surprising that he was able to provide the requisite historical depth and connect Rosenzweig to medieval Jewish philosophers. In 1982 Samuelson published his first, very short article using Rosenzweig's thought by pairing that with the philosophy of ibn Daud.[42] He used both of

---

[42] Norbert M. Samuelson, "Ibn Daud and Franz Rosenzweig on Other Religions: A Contrast between Medieval and Modern Jewish Philosophy," in *Proceedings of the Eighth World*

them to not only provide a Jewish perspective on other religions but also to demonstrate the differences in perspective between medieval and modern Jewish philosophies.

Another essay that critically explored the connection between Rosenzweig and his medieval antecedents was "Halevi and Rosenzweig on Miracles."[43] As is well known, Rosenzweig had translated Halevi's poetry in the 1920s as a way to aesthetically and thus existentially grasp and then situate the historical relationship of Jews to the dominant culture of that time.[44] This more complex existential significance of the work then becomes an index for the growth of Samuelson's political and cultural convictions and their intellectual expression. Samuelson drew out the existential relevance of Rosenzweig for modern Jews in his essay "On Reading Rosenzweig's *Star*," published in the semi-academic venue *Sh'ma* and demonstrating the commitment of Samuelson to Jewish education outside the academy.[45] Typical of his didactic style, the article begins by Samuelson's recounting a story of guiding a student on how to not only read *The Star of Redemption* but how to read any classical work in philosophy or literature in general. Samuelson notes that Rosenzweig's writing, while markedly original, is not especially difficult to understand. What most readers fail to bring to the reading of the text, however, and thus what most readers fail to bring to most readings of classical texts in philosophy (and not just Jewish philosophy), is an adequate knowledge of the background sources. According to Samuelson, "what makes it so difficult is not Rosenzweig's creativity, but our lack of background in his sources. The problem is that the post-World War Two college course requirements of an American are not the same as the pre-World War Two curriculum of a German. We do not know less than Rosenzweig. We simply know different things."[46]

Rosenzweig, of course, was not the only modern Jewish philosopher analyzed closely by Samuelson. Other thinkers—Baruch Spinoza, Hermann Cohen, Martin Buber, Mordecai Kaplan, and Emil Fackenheim—also received close attention as Samuelson engaged their ideas historically, criti-

---

Congress of Jewish Studies, Division C (Jerusalem: World Union of Jewish Studies, 1982), 75–80.

[43] Norbert M. Samuelson, "Halevi and Rosenzweig on Miracles," in *Approaches to Judaism in Medieval Times*, ed. David R. Blumenthal (Chico, CA: Scholars Press, 1984), 157–72.

[44] See Barbara E. Galli, *Franz Rosenzweig and Judah Halevi: Translating, Translations, and Translators* (Montreal: McGill-Queens University Press, 1995).

[45] Norbert M. Samuelson, "On Reading Rosenzweig's Star," *Sh'ma* 16, no. 316 (September 1986): 122–24.

[46] Ibid., 124.

cally, and constructively. Samuelson's distinctive contribution to modern Jewish philosophy has many facets: he explicates the ideas of outstanding thinkers and enables the reader to understand what they said; he engages them critically in order to determine what is viable in their rational exposition of Judaism; he absorbed their own ideas into his own constructive theology; he explores modern texts in light of science and mathematics in order to determine what is philosophically viable about their position, and he teaches how to read modern and contemporary Jewish philosophical texts as a guide for contemporary Jewish living. This engagement with modern thinkers is strikingly midrashic (that is, exegetical and dialogical), showcasing the nature of Jewish philosophy. Rosenzweig himself provided Samuelson with the model of doing Jewish philosophy in this manner. Put differently, Samuelson's engagement with Rosenzweig exemplifies Samuelsonian midrashic philosophical practice at its finest.

Constructive Jewish Theology:
The Dialogue of Science and Religion

Samuelson's distinctive style of writing blends history, criticism, and construction for a reason: how we reconstruct the past expresses our own views in the present and our vision for the future. From the study of the past texts (as interpreted by him) Samuelson takes what he considers to be the best explication of Jewish beliefs. This explication has to stand the test of believability: what is not believable because it is not true must not be affirmed, because God is truth. Judaism expresses many beliefs about God, the world, and the human, but these beliefs must always be subjected to scrutiny in light of what we know to be true from philosophy and science. The philosophic reconstructing and reinterpretation of Judaism is therefore ongoing and never ending: this is the task of Jewish philosophy. The moment Jewish philosophy relinquishes the task, Jewish philosophy will die and with it Judaism will wither or will become a form of idolatry. If it is to be resurrected, Judaism will have to be open to contemporary philosophy and science and will have to undergo a wholesale reinterpretation. This is the provocative message of *Jewish Faith and Modern Science: On the Death and Rebirth of Jewish Philosophy* (2009). The book reflects Samuelson's three decades of involvement in science and religion dialogue, an international conversation dominated by non-Jewish philosophers, theologians, and historians of science as well as his own study of science, especially physics. Since the mid-1990s he has published in *Zygon: Journal of Religion and Science*, the major academic venue of this discourse, contributed to anthologies and reference books,[47] and wrote several entries about Judaism and science for the *Encyclopedia of Sciences and Religions*, where he served as section editor.[48] The specific issues treated in *Jewish Faith and Modern Science* reflect the ongoing discussions he had at ASU since 2004 in seminars, conferences, and workshops.[49]

To understand why Samuelson argues that science is crucial for the survival of Judaism, it is important to begin by paying attention to semantics. Samuelson argues correctly that the term "science," in the sense of information about the physical world, was a modern invention. In the premodern world, "science" meant "knowledge," of which information about the physical world was just one aspect. Indeed, that information constituted what was known as "natural philosophy." If Jewish philosophy is necessary for the survival of Judaism, and if "science" is what was previously known as "natural philosophy," then science is part of Jewish philosophy. To be Jewishly informed, Jews must be scientifically informed and must apply their understanding of science to their interpretation of Judaism. In 2008 Samuelson and Elliot Dorff founded the Judaism, Science, and Medicine Group (JSMG), which is administered by the Center for Jewish Studies at Arizona State University. Through its annual conferences the organization has advanced the dialogue between Judaism, science, and medicine and has enhanced the interdisciplinary discourse between the humanities, the natural sciences, and the social sciences.[50]

Creation

How should one interpret Judaism in light of science? Samuelson began to address that question by turning first to the doctrine of creation, the key doctrine of Judaism and a central concern for Jewish philosophers. To launch the study of creation he first assembled a group of scientists,

---

[47] For example, Norbert M. Samuelson, "Three Comparative Maps of the Human," *Zygon: Journal of Religion and Science* 31, no. 4 (1996): 695–710; Norbert M. Samuelson, "Judaism and Science," in *The Oxford Handbook of Religion and Science* (Oxford: Oxford University Press, 2006): 41–56; Norbert M. Samuelson, "On the Symbiosis of Science and Religion: A Jewish Perspective," *Zygon: Journal of Religion and Science* 35, no. 1 (2000): 83–97; Norbert M. Samuelson, "Reflections on the Distinctness of Judaism and the Sciences," *Zygon: Journal of Religion and Science* 46, no. 2 (2011): 396–413.

[48] Anne L. C. Runehov and Lluis C. Oviedo, eds., *Encyclopedia of Sciences and Religions* (Dordrecht: Springer, 2013).

[49] See Samuelson, *Jewish Faith and Modern Science*, vii–viii.

[50] Information about the organization and its annual conferences is available on the website of Jewish Studies at ASU. See http://jewishstudies.clas.asu.edu.

Judaica scholars, and theologians to discuss the relevant conceptual challenges and to pose a potential trajectory for future research. The proceedings of that conference were published as *Creation and the End of Days: Judaism and Scientific Cosmology*,[51] establishing the conceptual connection between views of the world's origins and beliefs about the end. He then proceeded to study the rabbinic discourse on creation collected in Midrash Genesis Rabbah and subjected it to close analysis. The result was *The First Seven Days: The Philosophical Commentary on the Creation of Genesis*,[52] an analysis that paved the way to his later book *Judaism and the Doctrine of Creation*.[53] In order to write this book, Samuelson devoted time to study contemporary physics with the help of friend and physics professor at Indiana University, Donald Lichtenberg, and he published several essays on the doctrine of creation. The book is not only an attempt to reconstruct the doctrine of creation in Judaism but also a call for other Jewish philosophers to read Jewish sources in light of contemporary science.

As a philosopher who is attentive to history, one could have expected the book to be arranged chronologically, going from antiquity to the present as one normally does in historical surveys. But that is not the case. Rather, the organization of the book is determined by the logic of the argument about how Jewish philosophy should be done. The model for the book is Hermann Cohen's *Religion of Reason: Out of the Sources of Judaism*, whose claims, like Samuelson's, "are intended to be rational."[54] But instead of trying to be comprehensive of the entire gamut of Jewish tradition, Samuelson selects only a few primary sources, and instead of starting with the Hebrew Scriptures, Samuelson begins his rational exposition with Rosenzweig's *Star of Redemption*, since it "is the best contemporary example of creation as the doctrine of Jewish philosophy."[55] After discussing Rosenzweig, Samuelson goes back in time to explore the "Jewish roots of his view in medieval Jewish philosophy and in classical rabbinic philosophical commentaries," which leads him "to examine the sources for their views, viz.

---

[51] Norbert M. Samuelson and David Novak, eds., *Creation and the End of Days: Judaism and Scientific Cosmology* (Lanham, MD: University Press of America, 1986).

[52] Norbert M. Samuelson, *The First Seven Days: The Philosophical Commentary on the Creation of Genesis*, South Florida Studies in the History of Judaism 61 (Atlanta: Scholars Press, 1992).

[53] Norbert M. Samuelson, *Judaism and the Doctrine of Creation* (Cambridge: Cambridge University Press, 1994).

[54] Samuelson, *Judaism and the Doctrine of Creation*, 19.

[55] Ibid., 21.

Genesis and Plato's *Timaeus*."⁵⁶ Finally, in order to "judge the truth of what Jewish philosophy has to say about creation" he looks into "contemporary physics" and explains what it does best and where it fails. Out of this examination, Samuelson constructs what is the rational, "believable Jewish view of creation" and how to correctly understand the relationship between science and Judaism.

So what is a believable view of creation, according to Samuelson? The short answer is that creation (like redemption) is atemporal, it is not an event in time. Both creation and redemption, Samuelson says echoing Hermann Cohen, have to be understood as asymptotic processes that point toward the ideal and not to reality. Samuelson puts this most succinctly stating:

> No matter how far we look into the future, the end will never be reached; at best it can only be approximated. Similarly, no matter how far we look into the past, the origin can never be discovered; it too can only be approximated. As such both extremes are not themselves part of the actual processes of the universe. They are ideals that define actual experienced directions. As such, while the processes themselves are in space and time, their two terminal points are not. Consequently, both creation and redemption are atemporal.⁵⁷

This restatement of the Jewish view of creation emerges out of the very procedure of Jewish traditional texts that look to "contemporary relevant scientific and/or philosophical texts whose source of authority is eternal to the Jewish tradition" as Samuelson argues.⁵⁸ As the rabbis looked to Plato because they found him representing "the best scientific view of their time," contemporary Jews should consult the best science of our days, that is, physical cosmology.

Is there a difference between Plato and contemporary physical cosmology in terms of making creation believable? The answer is "a conditional yes."⁵⁹ In terms of depicting the actual processes of the universe, "contemporary physical cosmology provides us with the best tools yet developed for understanding creation,"⁶⁰ and therefore we should use it when we seek to understand the processes of the physical universe, as Samuelson attempts to show in chapter 7 of the book. However, contemporary physical cosmology is not adequate to deal with the question "is there a moral dimension

---

⁵⁶ Ibid.
⁵⁷ Ibid., 202–3.
⁵⁸ Ibid., 205.
⁵⁹ Ibid., 198.
⁶⁰ Ibid., 230.

to the universe?" In that regard, Plato and the rabbis who utilized his theories are more meaningful. The moral purpose of the universe cannot be addressed by science but only by philosophy of religion. Hence, the book ends with a discussion of "creation from the perspective of contemporary philosophy" where Samuelson returns to Rosenzweig not to restate his views but to critique them.

Rosenzweig's relational philosophy presented a "picture model of the dynamic universe as a Star of David [in Part III of *The Star*] [which] is beyond geometry."[61] Rosenzweig gets to this by using a form of midrash in Part II that enables him to bridge what he considered the inability of mathematics (a two-variable algebraic logic) to depict three-dimensional and dynamic reality. Rosenzweig's model—what he calls this "new relationship"—functions as a processional operation of thinking about the elements of reality (God, World, Human) as directional vectors moving from nothing to something, and is based on his adaptation of Hermann Cohen's infinitesimal calculus. Samuelson argues that Rosenzweig simply "overstated his case" in claiming that his New Thinking had overcome the Old Thinking of a two-variable Hegelian logic.[62] Instead, claims Samuelson,

> Rosenzweig's new "relations" or "interconnections" are asymptotic functions, i.e., two-dimensional curves from an infinite number of origins infinitesimally distant that extend towards an endlessly expanding limit... Rosenzweig was able to construct a model of what he thought was a new kind of geometry on which to model his "new thinking." We know that the geometry he had in mind is an instance of fractals. In fact the kind of fractal relevant to his new thinking is the Koch curve.[63]

In summing up his thinking on this, Samuelson says that while Rosenzweig came up with his model and claimed that it was "something beyond mathematical conception," the fact is that it was only beyond Euclidean geometry and linear algebra but not necessarily beyond mathematical conception. He goes on to point out that relating Rosenzweig's model of the Star of David to fractal geometry helps us to understand the reason why

---

[61] The pictorial nature of Rosezweig's philosophy is explained and illustrated most clearly in Samuelson, *Jewish Philosophy*, 315–21. Samuelson's explication of the visual dimension of Rosenzweig's philosophy reflects his own attunement to the visual arts. An avid lover of film and cinema, he has taught college-level courses on the image of Jews in films and has published several essays. See, for example, Norbert M. Samuelson, "A Serious Film" (a film critique of *A Serious Man* by E. and J. Coen), in *The Modern Jewish Experience in World Cinema*, ed. Lawrence Baron (Waltham, MA: Brandeis University, 2011), 294–302.
[62] Samuelson, *Judaism and the Doctrine of Creation*, 253.
[63] Ibid., 254.

Rosenzweig claimed that the "language" of mathematics was inadequate for depicting the dynamics of relations but that fractal geometry, at the end of the day, still relies on mathematics for its work. Samuelson then "argues against Rosenzweig's radical separation between what is knowable by science and philosophy on the one hand and by the study of revealed texts on the other."[64] The unique organization of the book is thus "an illustration how the two are not so radically separate and how the two should be interrelated;" in other words, the book is "an argument for the unity of reason and faith, science and religion."[65] Samuelson would coin the term *"religious science"*[66] to convey the originality of his approach to practicing Jewish philosophy. Whether Samuelson's book is a critique of Rosenzweig, as he argues, or rather a development of an alternative to Rosenzweig using the asymptotic logic of Rosenzweig, is a point that will engage experts of Rosenzweig as much as it continued to engage Samuelson's own constructive theology, when he focused his attention on the doctrine of revelation.

Revelation

The book *Revelation and the God of Israel* is the second of Samuelson's planned trilogy of books to explicate the core tenets of Judaism: creation, revelation, and redemption.[67] Although Samuelson indicates that the book should be read independently of his *Judaism and the Doctrine of Creation*, it quickly becomes apparent that this is not the case. The new project wrestles with a similar methodological question: "is the God of revelation believable?" Like creation, revelation qualifies as one of the "big questions" to which we seek answers. But there are obvious differences between the two beliefs. Whereas the belief in creation is limited to specific biblical and rabbinic texts, "revelation is a theme that runs across the entire Hebrew Scriptures and no single text has privileged status in terms of either detail or importance."[68] Talking about revelation in light of science is also very difficult because "there is no single science whose subject matter corresponds to revelation. Revelation is a relation between God and individual human beings in which communication takes place,"[69] but there is no one

---

[64] Ibid., 249.
[65] Ibid.
[66] Ibid., 246.
[67] Samuelson, *Revelation and the God of Israel* (Cambridge: Cambridge University Press, 2002).
[68] Ibid., 5.
[69] Ibid.

science that studies communication. Finally, determining what is reasonable and believable about revelation is much more difficult because the life sciences do not operate on the same epistemic level as physics and cosmology. Therefore, *Revelation and the God of Israel* considers the belief in divine revelation from multiple well-informed perspectives of evolutionary psychology, political ethics, analytic philosophy of religion, and the source-critical and form-critical analyses of the Bible. The doctrine of revelation requires us to move into the social sciences and the humanities, which are inherently more ambiguous and conceptually challenging than the physical sciences.

To provide what Samuelson calls a "believable concept of revelation," he has to get his readers to the point where they can accept the reasonability of the form of the relationship called "revelation" but based on the unintelligibility of the terms that constitute that relationship, that is, one that depends on accepting the nonliteral source of what may constitute what is called revelation from the Jewish tradition. To do so, Samuelson returns to Rosenzweig once again to convey this alternate form of revelation, namely, as one of the communication of an intense presence that solicits inspired response (or responsibility). The means that we have to take into this account are the phenomena of post-facto speech, pledge, and the responsa of obedience and service. Doing so calls for the ongoing tasks of translation between different languages of communities of meaning to get at the "universal" aspect of life, what for Samuelson, as for Rosenzweig, is otherwise referred to as the ultimate messianic state.

For Samuelson, whereas science in the context of creation informs knowledge, science in the context of revelation is only capable of providing interpretation, which then has to do with ethics and moral judgments. And making sense of those sorts of phenomena depends upon ascertaining the specific, historical languages of communities of meaning. True to this historical approach, Samuelson examines the biblical, rabbinic, medieval, and modern versions of the belief in revelation and he tests them against the most relevant sources of scientific knowledge, be it physical cosmology, evolutionary biology, philosophy of religion, or biblical criticism. Out of this conversation emerges the argument that a literal approach to biblical revelation is untenable as much as the medieval philosophical position is not viable because it depends on Aristotelian physics and metaphysics that have been proven obsolete. Newton and then Einstein made Aristotle's science inadequate as a description of the physical world, and Kantian critique debunked Aristotelian metaphysics. The only viable understanding of revelation is the modern view of revelation as an encounter, or relationship, and the best expositor of it, according to Samuelson, is Franz Rosenzweig. Moving away from the static cosmos of Aristotelian physics to the world of processes and vectors, as Samuelson explains in the book on creation, Rosenzweig was able to explain revelation as a dynamic relationship.

To believe in revelation, therefore, is to speak about *human response* to divine presence, not unlike the way that Buber interpreted revelation. In this understanding, God is not a personality that expresses commands in words, but rather a presence that is experienced. The collective response to that presence specifies the content of revelation.

To people familiar with modern Jewish philosophy, this understanding of revelation comes as no surprise, but Samuelson's attempt to prove it in light of evolutionary psychology is novel and welcome, although not all readers will find it compelling, because they may challenge Samuelson's own criteria of "believability."

Samuelson has continued to argue the case for making Judaism believable as a precondition for the survival of Judaism and as the primary task of Jewish philosophy. In the concluding sections of the book on revelation, Samuelson clearly states his contentious belief that there simply are no other Jewish philosophers after Rosenzweig in the twentieth century who wrote with such compelling creativity about the interface of the science of his day with Jewish belief and tradition:

> A constructive contemporary Jewish philosophy that is coherent with what Jewish philosophy was in the past ought to be a serious critical study of the interface of the general consequences for understanding the world, the human, and the divine (in Rosenzweig's terms) from contemporary empirical sciences with the tradition of Jewish texts, from the Hebrew Scriptures through modern Jewish thought (in Maimonides' terms). The goal is to formulate reasonable judgments about the viability of Judaism that are believable and have moral merit. This scholarly activity requires knowledge of relevant texts out of the religious history of the Jewish people as well as familiarity with the claims of contemporary sciences and the ways by which those claims are derived.[70]

Redemption

The third cardinal belief of Judaism, redemption, is the focus of Samuelson's current work and is not yet available in a monograph. However, he has written extensively about redemption in his most recent book, *Jewish Faith and Modern Science*. There he offers a systematic critique of contemporary

---

[70] Samuelson, *Jewish Philosophy*, 325.

Jewish philosophy and spells out the way to overcome a perceived crisis. The central claim of the book is that "modern Jewish philosophy does not understand modern science in every academic discipline of science relevant to what Jews believe as Jews."[71] The main target of the critique is the practitioners of Jewish philosophy as an academic discipline, namely, Samuelson's own professional cohorts in the academy. He divides them into two groups: the first "deals with classical texts that they call medieval Jewish philosophy, but these scholars rarely treat their objects of scholarship as philosophy."[72] Some of them are "historians of ideas who concern themselves with what their texts mean only enough to provide a surface interpretation, but never with the kind of probing by which these texts might continue to function, as they originally functioned, as part of a reasoned path leading to personal collective wisdom."[73] The other group consists of scholars "who study classical texts [as] archivists and philologists" and they "almost never ... discuss whether what the authors of these texts teach is true."[74] As Samuelson sees it, both groups are failing the task and mission of Jewish philosophy because they express no interest in establishing the truth of the texts they study. The lack of concern for truth is the cause of what he pronounces as the "death of Jewish philosophy"[75] and the sorry states of affairs of contemporary Judaism, especially the contemporary rabbinate that has lost its intellectual edge and its ability to engage in the pursuit of truth.

So long as practitioners of Jewish philosophy ignore or misunderstand contemporary sciences, they will continue to operate within an obsolete worldview which has been debunked by modern science or perpetuate defunct cultural categories, established in political structures that have long been replaced. In order to revive Jewish philosophy (and by extension, contemporary Judaism), a wholesale philosophic reexamination and reconstruction of Judaism is needed. This reconstruction is not to be undertaken apologetically by translating Judaic beliefs into scientific lingo (as some Orthodox participants in the science and religion dialogue have done) but rather in admitting that modern science poses serious challenges

---

[71] Samuelson, *Jewish Faith and Modern Science*, 12.
[72] Ibid., 231.
[73] Ibid.
[74] Ibid., 232.
[75] Samuelson first articulated the charge that Jewish philosophy is dead in his "Death and Revival of Jewish Philosophy," *The Journal of the American Academy of Religion* 70, no. 1 (2002): 117–34. The arguments of that essay were later developed in his *Jewish Faith and Modern Science*.

that compel Judaism to subject its beliefs to self-criticism in order to make Judaism believable.[76] When Judaism is so reconstructed, it could challenge contemporary science and expose its blind spots (especially reductionist materialism) and the arrogance involved in the ideology of scientism that glorifies secular atheism.[77] Unless Jewish philosophy undertakes this critical dialogue, Jewish philosophy will die; it will have no justification for continued existence. Samuelson boldly states:

> It is precisely these truth judgments that need to be the concern of twenty-first century Jewish critical thinking if Judaism is to reemerge as a believable (rather than merely comfortable, nostalgically satisfying) path of collective and individual well being. It is for these reasons that Jewish philosophy as it has been practiced in the last two-thirds of the twentieth century is dying as philosophy and deserves its fate.[78]

In short, Jewish philosophers today must not adhere to obsolete science or defend obsolete conceptions of God, the world, and humanity. To show how this work is to be done, Part I of the book offers a critique of contemporary Jewish philosophy from the perspective of several natural and social sciences (physics and astronomy, linguistics and epistemology, psychology, medicine, and history), whereas Part II presents "constructive suggestions for the agenda of future Jewish philosophy with respect to Jewish thought in general."[79]

The task of Jewish philosophy has become more urgent today because today's rabbis (unlike their ancient and medieval predecessors) have long given up on the pursuit of truth, lack requisite philosophical knowledge, and have no authority. As Samuelson puts it,

> The rabbis' claim for authority was based on the judgment that what they distinctly know was how to determine the true meaning of the Hebrew scriptures, and these scriptures serve as a foundational source for truth judgments about absolutely everything. The rabbis have lost their authority because Jews in the modern world do not believe either of these claims.[80]

---

[76] See Samuelson, *Jewish Faith and Modern Science*, 232–34. The list of challenges appears variously in other places of the book and in the essay "The Challenges of the Modern Sciences for Jewish Faith," *CCAR Journal* (Winter 2012): 12–27; this essay is included in this volume.

[77] Samuelson singles out Richard Dawkins as an exponent of this misguided scientism and subjects his views to scathing critique. See Samuelson, *Jewish Faith and Modern Science*, 161–62, 206–7 nn. 3–4; Norbert M. Samuelson, "A New Militant Atheism: Dawkins's *God Delusion*—A Review Essay," *CCAR Journal* (Fall 2010): 195–203.

[78] Samuelson, *Jewish Faith and Modern Science*, 232.

[79] Ibid., 102 n. 6.

[80] Ibid., 6.

The rabbis lost their credibility because rabbis do not have the best training to interpret the Scriptures and the Scriptures are no longer accepted as foundational for what is real and what is true. Modern Jews turn towards those who study nature—such as physicists, biologists, and psychologists who inform us about what is most reasonable to believe about the external and internal worlds—rather than to rabbis who study just the Scriptures. And even those academics who study archaeology, anthropology, and history are believed to know more about what the authors of the ancient Hebrew texts meant than contemporary rabbis who are trained to read the texts of the earlier rabbis, including the Hebrew Scriptures to the midrashim and the commentaries. In short, the "death of Jewish philosophy" is based on the modern state of contemporary human knowledge of the sciences and philosophy, that is, the methods of knowing anything whatsoever.

The issue, as Samuelson succinctly points out, is the difference between modern science and ancient forms of textual interpretation, or the hermeneutics and midrashic practices developed by the Jews. This even extends in many cases to moral authority, which means that modern science can better inform us about the environmental and behavioral conditions that can predict what would happen in actual cases of human beings that determine who they are and how they are by biological and social conditions, compounded in complexity by advances in the technological sciences in the second half of the twentieth century—genetics, robotics, information science, and nanotechnology (GRIN)—which may lead to a time in the very near future when humans will serve the interests of machines instead of machines serving human interests. In other words, human nature could change so radically that humans will no longer act as agents of change in the world.

So how are we to think properly about redemption? The answer was already intimated in his early work on creation, which noted that both the origin of the universe (i.e., creation) and its end (i.e., redemption at the end of time) are atemporal. They are infinite end points that can only be asymptotically approximated, but never reached. Samuelson explains that redemption "is a remote limit or goal toward which all of nature (both physical and mental) is directed in motion, and it is an end that will never be realized in space or reached in time. It is a real end, but its realization is infinitely remote."[81] Both creation and redemption are "acts that describe what God does, and since God is not subject to change, neither are creation

---

[81] Ibid., 177.

and redemption."[82] To understand this claim we need to think about divine action "as processes in the universe that must be understood asymptotically to be an expression of ideal ends. These ideals are never actually achieved. Still they function as goals for every existent creature with very created natural function."[83] Astrophysics can give us some clue about what the remote end will be: "things would be comparatively so remote from each other that it would seem that there is nothing at all; forces will be so relatively weak that they would seem not to exist at all, and the light in the universe now would be so dim comparatively as to not be light at all."[84]

In this total cosmic vision there is a difference between "the end of days" and the end of natural and human history, which the rabbinic tradition labeled as "Kingdom of God." The latter takes place in space-time and signifies emerging unification as "diverse motions of the nations of the earth come together in unity with God as one earth with one people in harmony for the first time with their creator."[85] However, in the absolute end (which rabbinic Judaism calls "the end of days"), "motions of everything into regions of light and dark are themselves overcome, and a final cosmic unity of everything is achieved."[86] In the absolute final end, the separation between humans and animals, the living and nonliving, the organic and the inorganic are finally overcome. For this reason, Samuelson is not at all perturbed by the fact that currently there are people who want to use science and technology to overcome natural human limitations through enhancement and genetic engineering. As far as Samuelson is concerned,

> there is no inherent reason to doubt that modern science can contribute technologies for human beings to enhance their life-long quest to become more than human, and to become transformed into servants of the Lord. However, I think that this goal cannot, even in principle, be achieved by creatures in this sensible world of extension in time and space.[87]

In the final pages of the book, Samuelson's critical engagement with contemporary science on the basis of Jewish sources poses a vision of reality that echoes a Whiteheadian process philosophy and a Rosenzweigian metaphilosophy (which he called the "New Thinking") because they are compatible with modern science. Maimonides was right to insist that the origin of

---

[82] Ibid., 179.
[83] Ibid.
[84] Ibid., 178–79.
[85] Ibid., 199.
[86] Ibid.
[87] Ibid., 192.

the universe (creation) is unknowable. Indeed, our universe comes from an unknowable origin (creation) and proceeds toward its unknowable end (redemption). This process of "endless motions from origins in nothing to ends as something of value is better understood in moral than in physical terms."[88] Drawing deeply from Rosenzweig's inspirational vision of a messianic redemption beyond all metaphysically conceivable worlds, Samuelson concludes his book saying:

> In the new thinking God is worshipped and served primarily as the ultimate end with which everything unites in an idealized anticipated conclusion to all history—mineral, vegetable, and animal no less than human and divine—in a singular state of unity that transcends all conceptual dichotomies, including Jews and the nations, humans and animals, life and death, and even creation and the creator. As such the logic of the new thinking is inherently ethical in purpose and utopian in nature rather than discursive in both nature and purpose.[89]

The revival of Jewish philosophy and of Judaism relies on the correct understanding of the nature of reality as well as the entire gamut of existence, including human existence (social, political, and economic). Such a view, however, is only available in modernity through science and not philosophy. What concerns Samuelson is that modern Jews have divorced their intellectual life from reflecting on the nature of the universe, focusing on politics (Zionism) and spiritual life (e.g., Neo-Hasidism) but not on science, as he advocates. What Samuelson bemoans is that while there is considerable intellectual commitment to understanding the relationship between ethical forms of Jewish life and medicine, that is, to bioethics, there is almost no intellectual activity between what it means to be Jewish and other forms of science. He understands his project as a constructive one, establishing new institutional patterns where Jewish intellectuals are informed by one or more modern sciences that then inform the training of new rabbis and their reading practices of traditional texts. Such an institutional reformation would extend over all forms of Jewish educational institutions, from Jewish schools for children to undergraduate and graduate curricula in secular academic institutions. This is Samuelson's constructive theology and, from his perspective, the only responsible and reasonable way forward for modern Jewish philosophy.

---

[88] Ibid., 236.
[89] Ibid.

The Essays That Follow

The four essays selected for this volume present Samuelson's approach to Jewish philosophy as a constructive project. The first essay, "A Critique of Rosenzweig's Doctrine: Is It Jewish and Is It Believable?," presents his view of creation. The essay, which was originally published as Chapter 2 of *Judaism and the Doctrine of Creation*, illustrates how Samuelson sets the test of believability and why Rosenzweig passes the test. The second essay, "The God of the Theologians," was originally published as Chapter 3 of *Revelation and the God of Israel* and illustrates the same procedure in regard to the doctrine of revelation. Focusing on Hermann Cohen and Martin Buber, the essay demonstrates how Samuelson both summarizes the views of past Jewish thinkers and engages them critically. Out of his critical engagement, which explicates what is problematic in a given thinker, Samuelson's own theology unfolds. The third essay, "The Concept of 'Nichts' in Rosenzweig's 'Star of Redemption,'" marks the beginning of Samuelson's engagement with Rosenzweig, and provides a clue as to why Rosenzweig has been so central to Samuelson's own constructive theology. The essay also bridges Samuelson's exposition of Maimonides' negative theology and his interpretation of Rosenzweig. The fourth and final essay, "The Challenges of the Modern Sciences for Jewish Faith," is a succinct summary of the specific challenges that modern science poses to the three tenets of Judaism, creation, revelation, and redemption and a programmatic call for Jews to engage in science in order to revive Judaism and Jewish philosophy.

In conclusion, Samuelson has written numerous books and essays that have a very consistent message: in order to survive, Judaism must be believable and to turn Judaism into a believable religion is the task of Jewish philosophy. Deeply attentive to history, Samuelson has presented Judaism and Jewish philosophy in particular as historical phenomena that have evolved through interaction with the surrounding civilizations. As a historical tradition, the canonic texts are themselves the product of human response to divine revelation as understood by the tools available in a given culture. In the twenty-first century that means that Judaism must reconstruct itself with the tools of contemporary science and in so doing it will not only ensure its own believability, but will also offer a critique either to the way philosophy is currently practiced in the academy or to the way religion is understood by the discipline of Religious Studies. As much as Samuelson invites Jews to reinterpret and reconstruct their own belief systems, he also calls on non-Jews to reexamine how they understand categories such as "religion" or "philosophy." This critical engagement should always be carried out in the historical context, since human beings are temporal historical creatures. Samuelson's approach to Judaism and to Jewish philosophy reveals his ongoing indebtedness to liberal Judaism, namely, the emphasis on beliefs and ideas over ritual and praxis, and the attentiveness to historical development. The project of explicating and testing Judaism's truth claims throughout history is not inherently political but it has ramification for contemporary Judaism especially in terms of the challenge to rabbinic authority. For Samuelson, a Judaism that worships either obedient praxis and conformist dogma or emotional spirituality and fuzzy thinking will fail to survive and will have no right to survive. Only a Judaism that integrates philosophy, science, religion, and faith will be viable for the future.

A CRITIQUE OF ROSENZWEIG'S DOCTRINE: IS IT JEWISH AND IS IT BELIEVABLE?

Norbert M. Samuelson

The discussion of the concept of creation out of the sources of Judaism began with modern Jewish philosophy. In this instance only two notable Jewish thinkers address the question with any degree of depth, Nachman Krochmal and Franz Rosenzweig. Except for the fact that the latter seems to have been influenced by the former, for our purposes there is no connection worth mentioning between them. In terms of development and depth of analysis, both with respect to philosophy and theology, there is no comparison. Clearly Rosenzweig's statement is the more important of the two. Hence, the descriptive part of the first section of this study (viz., creation in modern Jewish philosophy) focused almost exclusively on what Rosenzweig wrote. That discussion broke down into two parts—Rosenzweig's philosophy and Rosenzweig's theology.

The two parts of Rosenzweig's discussion of creation differ radically in their mode of presentation. The first is a philosophic analysis built upon his understanding of the history of philosophy. The second is a linguistic commentary on the Hebrew scriptures. However, the conception of creation that emerges through the two disciplines is a single view that in itself shows why Rosenzweig discussed the question in the way that he did. Creation is a philosophic/scientific concept that points to the insufficiency of both philosophy and theology to understand the origin of the universe. Its conception begins as a philosophical question but its solution lies beyond the scope of purely logical empirical thinking. Creation must be grasped as something that is revealed through the word of God as recorded in scripture. Hence, while creation begins as a philosophic doctrine, it ends as a theological dogma.

With respect to philosophy, creation expresses one of three dimensions of relations that determine the dynamic character of reality. Each of these dimensions is itself something dynamic. They are best understood in the same way that their occupants are, viz., as vectors whose direction is from an origin to an end, where the vectors' limits at both extremes are themselves vectors that function with respect to the dimensions they define as

---

This chapter was first published in *Judaism and the Doctrine of Creation,* by Norbert M. Samuelson. Copyright © 1994 by Cambridge University Press. Reprinted with permission.

asymptotes. In the case of creation, the origin is God and the end is the world.

With respect to theology, creation is the first dimension of reality in the sense that it is the conceptual foundation of the other two dimensions. God's creation of the world, in its movement towards its end, overlaps God's revelation to man, whose own end overlaps man's redemption of the world. A God who is barely God (divine spirit) barely acts (hovers) over a unified universe (heaven and earth) that is really nothing at all (viz., an empty waste that is darkness); this negativity becomes minimally positive (light) as a passive object (space) that, through differentiation, leads through the generation of a series of substantive objects to the creation of man who, as an entity capable of hearing and speaking, becomes more than a mere object, a mere creature. The capacity for speech changes divine spirit into God and transforms (at least some) creaturely objects (viz., humans) into persons. But God as commander and human as person transcend creation. It points to the relationship that the trans-objective God and human define, viz., the path or way of revelation.

At this point I hope I have succeeded in showing that Rosenzweig's doctrine of creation is both intelligible and coherent. However, at this stage a critical reader ought to ask, what makes this view Jewish and why would anyone give credence to Rosenzweig's story. In the remainder of this chapter I will explain what these two questions involve. The next three parts of this book will attempt to answer them.

Issues of Jewishness

Much of the basis for denying that Rosenzweig's concept of creation is Jewish has been mentioned in the discussion of his theology. Simply stated, Rosenzweig's theory seems to have more in common with Greek philosophy, notably Plato's *Timaeus*, than it does with either biblical faith or the beliefs of the classic rabbis. To be sure, Rosenzweig's creation is not identical with Plato's account of the origin of the universe. The most notable difference is that, while both use mathematical tools to construct their models, the mathematics are radically different. Plato's universe begins with positive numbers that express figures in plate geometry. Conversely, Rosenzweig's universe is understood in terms of vector analysis and calculus. The former yields a picture of a static world of eternal objects, while the latter affirms a dynamic universe of endless intentional processes. At the same time the similarities between the two pictures are apparent.

Most notably, Rosenzweig's primordial universe in relation to its primordial deity seems more like Plato's receptacle under the influence of necessity than it does like the heaven and earth that God creates in the biblical text. How can a view that seems to be so Greek and so non-Hebrew be called a "Jewish" conception of creation?

In a word, the answer is, because Rosenzweig's view grows directly out of the analysis of creation in classical (medieval) rabbinic philosophy and in the rabbi's commentaries on the first chapter of Genesis. The demonstration of this thesis will be the subject matter of the second part of this book.

Issues of Interpretation

At this point it should be objected that even if Rosenzweig's account is Jewish in the sense that it agrees with, and was influenced by, rabbinic tradition, that does not mean that it is what the biblical text in fact says. This is no trivial claim. Rosenzweig's interest in interpreting the Hebrew scriptures is not merely the interest of a literary critic or a historian of ideas. For him the scriptures are revelation, and as such they are important for determining truth. Furthermore, as I argued in the introduction, the validity of Rosenzweig's reading of the text of Genesis is important for our concern with truth as well. As a Jew I take seriously what Jewish tradition has to say about everything. Part of that tradition is classical rabbinic literature. But the foundation of that literature is the Hebrew scriptures. Now, the entire tradition need not be coherent. If the way that the rabbis read scripture differs from what scripture says, that in itself is important, and, independent of the testimony of the rabbis, there is reason to believe that what Rosenzweig says the biblical text says is not what it says. Most notably, Rosenzweig's interpretation is questionable in two major respects. First, his interpretation of critical terms in the Genesis narrative does not seem to be what those words in fact mean in their biblical context. In general Rosenzweig seems to make them far more sophisticated and complex than they are in fact. Put simply, God's spirit hovering over water in a world that is empty, waste and dark means simply that. It does not tell us anything about an implicit ontology of a universe that is negative and passive. In other words, few readers of the Bible will recognize terms such as "God," "world" and "man" as Rosenzweig discusses them. For most people—be they Jewish or Christian, philosophers, theologians or laypersons—these words name objects, and not (as Rosenzweig would claim) dimensions. Similarly, "light" is light, "good" is good, and "man" is man. The text says nothing about the nature of attributes or the relation between creation and revelation. Put simply, what Genesis 1 describes is the God of the world who at a particular moment in time brings into existence the world out of absolutely nothing, then wills into existence the occupants of that world, including the first human being whose name is "Adam." That is all it says. Anything more found in the story is in the mind of the interpreter and not in the mind of the author(s) of the biblical text. In the words of nineteenth-century biblical criticism, it is an exercise in "eisegesis," not "exegesis." In other words, the attempt to turn a biblical story into a philosophical statement is in itself a distortion of the text. Hence, how can a view that is so philosophical be seriously considered a viable interpretation of the Genesis account of creation?

The third part of this book is intended to be an answer to this question. There I will look in some detail at both critical texts involved here (viz., Plato's *Timaeus* and the first chapter of Genesis). I will argue for the viability of using the schema presented in Plato's account of the origin of the universe to conceptualize the cosmology and ontology implicit in the Torah's narrative about creation. Furthermore, I will argue that both works of ancient literature involve a similar understanding of what is the epistemological status of judgments about the origin of the universe and what is the style of thinking appropriate to discussing this question, viz., the use of a cosmological narrative or (in Plato's language) "myth."

Issues of Truth

The most difficult set of questions is left for last. Even if we grant that Rosenzweig's conception of creation is Jewish in the sense that it grows out of and is coherent with the traditional texts of Jewish philosophy, and even if we grant that it is a viable interpretation of the biblical account of creation, why should we believe it to be true? There are a number of features of Rosenzweig's view that stand in marked opposition to the way that most of us (who are the products of twentieth-century European/American culture, whether we be philosophers or scientists or laypersons) think about our origin.

First, Rosenzweig posits that at first the universe is uniform and then, through divine will, becomes diverse. In other words, basically what God does is takes a unified universe and makes it diverse. Consequently, difference rather than unity expresses God's will. In contrast, most contemporaries at least share this much in common with Hegelian philosophy—they agree that unity is better than diversity, so that if there is a God and God governs the world, then he values unity over diversity, so that the world ought to become more and not less, a single universe.

Second, Rosenzweig presents an ontology in which space is prior to relations in space which are prior to the terms of the relations. In other words, space is prior to actions and actions are prior to objects. Most of us consider the exact opposite order to be simple common sense. First and foremost there are substantive, objective things. These things enter into relations with other things, and it is the things that define the relations. Furthermore, things in relationship are located in space, but space is merely a way of relating things; in itself it is not anything at all.

Third, it seems to be common sense to claim that things either are or are not, absolutely, but it is not intelligible to speak about things being more or less. In other words, affirmations in ontology admit of only two values, being and not-being, and these values are discrete. In contrast Rosenzweig affirms a universe in which being and not-being constitute a continuum that admits of infinite degrees.

Fourth, Rosenzweig's reality is more negative than positive; in contrast, it seems common sense to believe that what is is something, and what is not is not anything at all. In other words, whatever reality is, it is something positive.

Fifth, Rosenzweig's universe has moral value built into it. The consequence of such a view is that a science that is valueless (i.e., morally neutral), is not capable of giving a sufficient account of reality. In contrast, most people today believe that, at least in principle, modern empirical science can give an adequate account of reality, which entails that in reality the universe is a-moral.

The concluding part of this book will attempt to defend Rosenzweig's position in all five of these instances. In doing so, Rosenzweig's doctrine of creation will be scrutinized in the light of contemporary physics. However, this is not to say that I will agree with everything that Rosenzweig says. For example, I want to argue against his radical separation of philosophy and reason from theology and revealed faith. This critique will be presented in the conclusion of this book where I look explicitly at the *method* for doing philosophy of religion that is implicit in this study.[1]

---

[1] Some friends urged me to write a prolegomena to this book on epistemology and methodology. I have resisted their suggestions. In part this is because I am more interested in ontology than epistemology and in trying to reach some theological conclusions than in discussing how it is possible to reach them. Also, since my way of doing philosophy of religion and Jewish philosophy differs significantly from the kinds of approaches that are currently fashionable, I want first to illustrate my approach and only then discuss its viability.

THE GOD OF THE THEOLOGIANS

Norbert M. Samuelson

The Discreditation of Rationalist Theology

The primary goal of this book is analysis and critique of the concept of revelation, as a philosophic concept, out of the sources of rabbinic Judaism. Revelation is to be understood at its most general level as a relationship between humans, as the recipients, and God, as the transmitter, of revealed information. In the case of Judaism, where the humans involved are the Jewish people, the term applied to the information is "Torah." Hence, the concept of revelation in Judaism builds on four other concepts—God, the human, the Jewish people, and the Torah. Of the four, my focus so far has been on the concept of God. The discussion has included the other three concepts as well, because they are all conceptually interrelated in Jewish belief, but the focus, at least for now, has been on the purported entity from which the revealed information originates. This kind of historically grounded, philosophic thinking about God is called "theology."

Maimonides as the Benchmark of Jewish Theology

Classical Jewish, rabbinic, philosophical theology does not end with Maimonides. On the contrary, the tradition continues, without disruption, to the present day, without any indication of an end. However, for present purposes, where the focus is on the notion of God as it relates to revelation, Jewish philosophy (perhaps even philosophy in general) reached its highest development with Maimonides. Others, such as Gersonides, will modify Maimonides' views. Still others, from Crescas[1] through Spinoza,[2] will offer major philosophical critiques of Maimonides' view. Yet, what Maimonides said about the God of Torah remains the benchmark for all Jewish thinking about God—be it late medieval, early modern, modern, and postmodern. Some advocate his enterprise and others critique it, but the origin of all their own theology is Maimonides' writings about God.

This chapter was first published in *Revelation and the God of Israel*, by Norbert M. Samuelson. Copyright © 2002 by Cambridge University Press. Reprinted with permission.

[1] Chasdai ben Judah Crescas, born in Barcelona around 1340, lived much of his life in Saragossa. Died 1410/11.

[2] Baruch Spinoza, 1632–1677, lived most of his life in Amsterdam.

Post-Rambam Critiques of Maimonides

Kabbalah

Imagination versus Intellect

The major critique of Jewish philosophy after Maimonides comes not from the philosophers but from the Jewish mystics, the Kabbalists. Many of the best and most inquisitive Jewish intellectuals in the centuries following Maimonides turn to Kabbalah rather than to philosophy for their investigation of the meaning of the Hebrew Scriptures, and they do so in a way that is entirely alien to Maimonides' philosophical quest—they use their imaginations in order to picture in visual terms God's nature, the nature of the world, the nature of humanity, and the relationship between them. Of these works the most influential is the *Zohar*, which, either intentionally or unintentionally, stands in direct opposition to practically everything Maimonides says. From a philosophical perspective, the most critical challenge from Kabbalah is its affirmation of the epistemic value of imagination over intellect.

Undergirding Maimonides' entire enterprise was the first conviction, rooted in the success of the Aristotelian natural philosophy or science of his day, that thinking about the truth of what our religion commands us to believe must be based on rational speculation rather than creative imagination. Through imagination we can become aware of all that is possible, but the realm of the possible far exceeds the domain of the actual, and imagination in itself provides us with no guidelines to distinguish the possible from the actual. As such, reason alone cannot lead us to the truth assumed to be embedded in the Torah. Reason and only reason provides the only natural tool available to human beings to understand divine revelation.

The Philosophical Critique of Aristotelian Reason

The confidence that Maimonides had in reason, which he shared with Muslim intellectuals of his time (notably Ibn Sina [Avicenna] and Ibn Rushd [Averroes]) undergoes sharp, critical attack in subsequent generations—especially from Al-Ghazali (1058–1111) against Ibn Sina near Maimonides' own time and from Crescas against Maimonides and Gersonides in later generations (1340–1411). The details of their arguments are not important here. I will only briefly summarize certain relevant conclusions.

The Aristotelians affirmed reality, at least within the sublunar world, as a complex of entities, called "substances," which themselves were concrete individuals, locatable in and moving through space and time. What constituted these substances as real was their individuality, identifiable by their singular spatial-temporal location. This physical identity was attributable to a principle called "matter." Matter made substances material, that is, it accounted for their materialization in reality, but it did not address what they are. What they are consisted not in what made them unique but in what made them like other substances. To know what an individual is is to define it, and definition consists in noting formal characteristics that the individual shares in common with other substances (the genus) as well as formal characteristics that distinguish the individual from the other members of its genus (the specific difference). However, the definition in general deals only with formal characteristics, with forms, and forms are in principle general, because what defines any form (as well as any complex of forms) is that it can exist in many places at the same time. Hence, forms, which render substances intelligible, are always universal, and, as such, are not real. Consequently, through reason we can know what something is, for we can grasp its formal nature, that is, we can grasp the constituent forms of a thing. However, we cannot in this way grasp the reality of the thing as something materialized in space and time as a distinct individual. Reality is material and individual, while philosophical-scientific-logical thought (reason) is always immaterial (or, formal) and general (or, abstract). Therefore, what we can know through reason is never real, and, given the Aristotelian commitment to a correspondence theory of truth, never true. Truth is in principle unknowable, at least through reason.

Maimonides' argument against relying on imagination and the senses to probe the meaning of the revealed word of God in the Hebrew Scriptures was that it could not yield truth, whereas through reason truth was (at least in part) discoverable. However, it turns out that the confidence (however qualified) of these philosophers in reason has rationally, that is, on its own terms, no foundation. To trust reason turns out not to be reasonable. Why not then, it can be argued, return to the use of imagination, which at least has the virtue of enabling us to think in ways broader than those our senses suggest from lived experience, which we know to be at best an inadequate picture of reality?

This is precisely what those Kabbalists did who asked the same kinds of theoretical questions that the philosophers asked (notably about God, the human, the world, and how the three are related). Whereas Maimonides took statements about the divine body to be non-material metaphors, the Kabbalists extended and radicalized these statements in order to picture in detail what God's body looked like, including his/her genitals,[3] and how

---

[3] See Elliot Wolfson, *Through A Speculum That Shines: Vision and Imagination in Medieval Jewish Mysticism* (Princeton: Princeton University Press, 1994).

both the universe and the human were images of the corporeal divine being.

Modern Science

While the growth of Kabbalah itself took the inadequacies of the Maimonidean presuppositions in one new direction, early European science took it in another direction. The notion of what is rational thinking itself began, in the late medieval and early modern period in western Europe, to break out of the restraints of the ancient Greek and Roman natural philosophy, as it evolved into the philosophic presuppositions about reality that are taken for granted in modern science. The development of the philosophical system presupposed in the modern scientific method reached its classic form in the seventeenth- and eighteenth-century writings of the natural philosophers René Descartes (1596–1650), Baruch Spinoza (1632–1677), Gottlob Leibniz (1646–1716), Isaac Newton (1642–1727), and, most notably, the French Positivists.[4] There are important differences between all of these thinkers, but for present purposes what they share in common is more important, because that common philosophical position, accepted as it stands, undercuts everything that Maimonides, and therefore Jewish philosophy, had to say about the philosophical God of the Hebrew Scriptures. It has to do with what they shared in their understanding of mathematics, logic, linguistics, and ontology.

New Philosophic Presuppositions: Positivism and the Ideal of Mathematical Precision

In a few words, whereas Aristotelian natural philosophy affirmed the reality of the negative and the vague as well as the positive and the precise, increasingly the new science affirmed that only what is positive and only what is precise can be real. With respect to ontology, the definitions of Aristotelian substances had (in modern terms) "fuzzy borders." In part, that is because the terms for the definitions were taken from ordinary language, which, as a reflection of ordinary usage, is unavoidably vague. But the vagueness was deeper than just language, for the imprecision of the language was seen to reflect the imprecision of reality, imprecision whose source was the notion of matter. Mathematical entities, such as numbers or geometric shapes, can have precise definitions, because they are no more than their definitions, which, as such, exist in logical thought but not in material reality. Once materialized, the precision vanishes, because matter itself is unde-

---

[4] Such as Auguste Comte (1798–1857).

finable. In contrast, the modern positivist philosophers insisted that what is real exists at any precise moment in a precise place, and that all these individuals—the moments, the places, and the things that occupy them— can be expressed clearly and distinctly, because each exists as something discrete.

The same is true of logic. The scientific language of Aristotelian logic was ordinary language that, as such, contained all the vagaries that arise from being "ordinary." The new scientific language (as it was finally formalized in written symbols at the beginning of the twentieth century), however, reflected a form and logic more in common with algebra than with literature. It assumed two kinds of terms, non-capitalized letters to name concrete individuals, and capitalized letters to express their general properties. Copulas were abandoned. Instead you had sentences in which the individuals and their properties were next to but not incorporated into each other. This language was seen to reflect a reality in which individuals are real and their properties are not, so that the relationship between them is external and purely conceptual. Names of individuals had references but not meanings, and meanings were concepts that had no proper material existence. Furthermore, the ultimate conceptual expressions about these existent, material, discrete individuals were algebraic statements, which were viewed to be the sole bearers of meaning and the only things that have truth value. Sentences have meaning and can be true or false; names for things only have reference, and the things referred to have neither meaning nor value.

Calculus and Infinity

What is perhaps most important about the new scientific thinking is that its model was mathematical, or, more precisely, algebraic. What is most important about it, for present purposes, is that the new language of logic with its entailed new philosophy solved the riddle of infinity. It provided us with a formalism—calculus—to make sense out of real infinities. First, it discovered many different kinds of infinity. (In part the problem of medieval discussions of infinity was that it assumed that all infinities are of the same kind.) Second, it used one fairly simple kind of infinity (viz., infinite series with a finite limit) to make sense out of locomotion, which, in contrast to alteration, is continuous, which seems to mean change through an infinite number of real points on a finite spatially conceived line.

The Problems with Maimonides' Theology

All of these changes in scientific thinking played a critical role in undermining the authority of Jewish philosophy, especially its theology. I have already alluded to the most important challenges. Two in particular need to be emphasized. First, in terms of mathematics, Maimonides' analysis assumes that because infinity names an endless process nothing actual can be infinite. However, all motion between two points in space is an infinite transition towards a finite limit and the limit, which is both rational and intelligible, expresses the real actuality of the infinite process. In fact all interesting applications of physical mechanics involving measurements of real things, such as areas or volumes of actual physical bodies, are instances of infinite change in the direction of finite limits, where the infinitely distant limits are the expression of the measurable reality of the things studied. Hence, the presumed fact that God is infinite in every respect does not mean that God is unknowable. On the contrary, he is humanly knowable through a logic, modeled on calculus, of ideal limits.

Second, logical expressions of the sort that can be judged true and false state, as they did for Aristotle, relations between subjects and predicates, but the predicate expressions are the sole conveyers of meaning that stand in an external relationship of predication to individual subjects that, in and of themselves, have reference but no meaning. Hence, relations between predicates and subjects do not entail complexity in the subjects, because the relations are external. However, all of Maimonides' arguments against literally affirming properties of God presupposed internal predication, where the term predicated of the subject God is understood to assert that God contains within his nature some attribute with which he is not identical. Given this new and improved logic, there is no apparent reason to restrict language about God to mere story telling.

Hermann Cohen

The philosopher of Judaism who first dealt seriously with the impact of modern science and philosophy on understanding the theology of the rabbinic literature, including the writings of Maimonides, was Hermann Cohen. His initial distinction was as interpreter of the philosophy of Immanuel Kant.

The Philosophy of Immanuel Kant

Kant had written three major critiques—a first of what he called "pure reason" (reinen Vernunft), a second of practical reason, and a third of aesthetics. In subject matter Kant's pure reason is close to what I have identified in Aristotle as theoretical reason. It is that rational activity that formulates conceptual knowledge from sense experience whose principles are what we human beings understand as physics and the other physical sciences. However, the two are not identical. For the Aristotelians these principles are ultimate principles of the universe; not so for Kant. He followed in a tradition of philosophy and science that had both absorbed the Muslim and Jewish critiques of Aristotelian science and moved beyond them to new, more mechanical rational philosophies, such as Descartes', and new more mathematical positivist sciences such as that of Newton. Kant no longer could make the same general claims for the epistemic authority of theoretical/pure reason that the Aristotelians had made. Like his ancient and medieval predecessors, Kant believed that this kind of reason yields certain objective knowledge, but it is not knowledge of reality. Kant therefore made a distinction between what is objective—views shared in common by all right-thinking human beings—and what is real. Pure reason, being dependent on the data of sense experience, can only tell us what is universally true of the world of empirical experience, but this world, although it is objective, is not reality. To understand reality requires a different kind of thinking, which he called "practical," as did the ancients, but we call "moral." This change is the most notable break with the epistemology of the Aristotelians, and it is a change that reflects the changes in thought about thinking that Maimonides and those who followed him expressed in terms of ethics.

I have already noted that the ambiguity of the Aristotelians on the question of whether human happiness has more to do with theoretical or with practical reason expresses itself in Jewish philosophy as an ambiguity over the nature of prophecy and human happiness.[5] All of the Jewish thinkers identify happiness as the moral end of human existence, associate its achievement with the attainment of happiness, and affirm, in line with Plato, that wisdom is of two sorts—theoretical (viz., the highest and most general truths of science) and practical (viz., judgments about how to live well [ethics] and how to guide others to live well [politics]). The question is, which is higher? In general, at the highest levels of wisdom, where humans become prophets and seem to be able to realize at least the horizon of the line that separates humanity from divinity, the distinction between the two kinds of wisdom disappears. In other words, the ultimate end towards

---

[5] See Howard Kreisel, *Maimonides' Political Thought: Studies in Ethics, Law, and the Human Ideal* (Albany: State University of New York Press, 1999), and Kenneth Seeskin, *Searching for a Distant God: The Legacy of Maimonides* (New York and Oxford: Oxford University Press, 2000).

which the human tends is to become, at least ideally, what Plato called a "philosopher king" and the Jewish Aristotelians called "prophets," whose practical thinking flows directly from their theoretical knowledge. In this sense, ethics—the study of what ought to be—transcends science—the study of what is, because at its highest level science becomes ethics.

It is in the spirit of this tradition of western thinking that Kant saw practical reason to be beyond pure reason. The domain of pure reason is scientific thinking, which gives us knowledge of, but only of, the world of sense experience, which Kant calls "phenomena." Beyond it is reality, which Kant calls "noumena." The realm of the noumena is the domain of God and his kingdom, which are both to be grasped, not with the discursive logic of science, but with a new, imperative logic of ethics. If this move is successful, Kant has brought philosophy and religion beyond the story-telling, myth-making stage of the rabbis. They rightly told stories, because they knew that their logic and their sense data were insufficient to inform them of the ultimate truths of God and his kingdom.

Cohen's Jewish Philosophy

The question is whether Kant succeeded. The major, intuitive problem for most of us is his seemingly peculiar claim that in knowing what ought to be true we know what really is true. Most people tend to think that ethics may tell us what is right and wrong, but it is powerless to inform us about what is and is not true. Hermann Cohen thought that Kant was right, and first wrote commentaries on Kant's three critiques and then constructive philosophical works of his own—on philosophy of science, on ethics, and on aesthetics—to demonstrate what he thought to be Kant's correct and conceptually revolutionary insights. Finally, he applied his philosophical discoveries to the study of religion in general and to rabbinic Judaism in particular, for he believed that rabbinic Judaism was already, especially on Maimonides' reading of it, the embodiment of Kantian philosophy. In other words, Cohen used Kant to reconstruct the Jewish philosophy of the Maimonideans as they had used Aristotle to reconstruct the Judaism of the Hebrew Scriptures and the early rabbis of the Midrash.

Cohen used the mathematical notion of the finite limited infinite series as a model for picturing reality. The phenomena are the series, and the noumena are the limit, where the series expresses actuality and the limit is the ideal that is identical with reality. God is presented primarily as the ideal end, analogous numerically to the number one, towards which the lived world, whose origin as creation is analogous numerically to the number zero, tends. History, human as well as natural, is a movement of integration from the nothing of creation towards the single something that is the unity of God with the world. Both the Torah and the classical rabbinic literature express this fundamental insight about the nature of reality in language guided practically to lead ordinary human beings towards their own understanding of this ultimate truth.

The theology of Cohen was a theology of a liberal progressive Judaism that affirmed the values of body Judaism and western European modernism and sought to synthesize the two into a coherent whole. Cohen provided such a synthesis. There is no question that, from the perspective of intellectual history, Cohen is one of the great philosophers, certainly one of the great Jewish philosophers. However, his appeal is limited solely to those who initially accept the values of both Judaism and modernism. Few outside the camp of progressive Judaism did. Non-Jews as well as assimilated Jews rejected the asserted values of rabbinic Judaism, and other Jews rejected the asserted values of modernism. The rejection of many of the values of modernism—rationality and individual autonomy being most critical among them—became strong, at least among European intellectuals, after the First World War. They tended, rightly or wrongly, to take the senselessness and brutality of that war as a *reductio ad absurdum* of the values, most apparent at least for Jews in the philosophy of Spinoza, that produced the modern, secular nationalist, capitalist, democratic nation state. These intellectuals were attracted more to forms of socialism—fascism, anarchism, and communism—than they were to the verbalized political ideals of the French and American revolutions; their Jewish counterparts were drawn more to a search for a new kind of Jewish religious spiritualism, even traditionalism, than they were attracted to forms of liberal Judaism.

Beyond Cohen

I will focus attention on two of these postmodern Jewish theologians, both of whom were deeply influenced by Cohen's thought in almost every respect except one—his modernist, rationalist liberalism. They are Martin Buber and Franz Rosenzweig. Buber and Rosenzweig were not disciples in the sense that they actually studied with Cohen. One did (Rosenzweig), but not the other (Buber). Nor were they Cohen's disciples in that they were his spokesmen. Rosenzweig had a political theory, but he did not advocate any form of political ideal for the world. Rather, he saw human salvation in religious communities, Jewish and Christian, instead of in secular politics. Buber, in contrast, remained his entire life a believer in the political process and a sort of utopian, but his political idealism was closer to the anarchist-agrarian vision of Tolstoy than to the mercantile-republican ideal of Locke and Jefferson. Buber was an active Zionist his entire life, first in Germany and then in Israel. Rosenzweig, in contrast, used his practical wisdom to create a small Jewish worshiping and studying community in Frankfurt.

The focus in this part of the book is on Buber's and Rosenzweig's conception of the God of revelation. In stating it I will have to speak of more than just their views of God, because what both say about the deity is inseparable from what they say in general about the world, the human, and the relationship between the three. Their view on the God of revelation is not cleanly separable from their views of revelation. However, again, my focus in this part is on their views of God. I will expand on their views of the human (the second term of the relationship that defines revelation) and revelation later.

Martin Buber

The three most important philosophical influences informing Buber's conception of God were Maimonides, Cohen, and (by means of Cohen) Immanuel Kant. The influences are both positive and negative. Buber accepts much that Maimonides said, but what he rejected in Maimonides is no less important. The same applies to the influence of Kant and Cohen. Those influences constitute the presuppositions of Buber's theology.

Presuppositions

From Maimonides

In agreement with Maimonides, the God of revelation is no less the God of creation, so that what we believe about the revealer must be consistent with what we believe about the creator. Clearly the creator is radically different from anything created, and God creates everything that exists in any way. Hence, there can be no human knowledge of God in any literal sense. Human knowledge consists of conceptual objects inferred from sense experience, and there can be no objective experience of anything that has not been created by God. However, this negative component of theology cannot be understood in the radical way that Maimonides presented it, for such a view of God the creator is incompatible with a deity who also reveals himself to human beings. There must be some way that

God can be known even though that way cannot be literally through grasping conceptual objects.

From Kant

In agreement with Kant, the universe can be divided into phenomenal and noumenal realms. We are knowing subjects who experience a world of objects and relations whose source lies in an interaction between our minds and something else. The domain of scientific knowledge is limited to phenomena. Phenomena are the world that our experience and logical reasoning inform. However, logical reasoning cannot tell us about the something else beyond phenomena, except that there is more to reality than phenomena. That something else—what Kant called "noumena"—is somehow knowable, for otherwise we would not be aware that there is something else, but it is not knowable in the same way that we know phenomena. It must be knowable in some other way.

Kant believed that the "other way" is moral reasoning. He developed a logic of practical wisdom (to use the terminology of classical Jewish philosophy) which in many respects paralleled the logic of theoretical wisdom. Both logics express universal value claims. The theoretical claims are expressed as declarative sentences whose values are either true or false; the practical claims are expressed as imperatives whose values are either good or bad. Both kinds of claims are "universal" in the sense that they are rules that apply to everything within their domain, but the domains are different. The values of theoretical logic range over all states of affairs involving objects in the world, while the values of practical logic range with equal unqualified universality over acts of will by knowing subjects. Buber presupposed all of this philosophy, except for two claims—Kant's judgment that ethics are about a noumenal reality divorced from the empirical world of lived life, and Kant's claim of universality for moral judgments.

Ethics applies to the lived life of individual conscious entities—human beings—in their lived relations with other individual conscious entities in the phenomenal world. An ethics such as the one that Kant proposes could have no practical application in such real life. Moral judgments are not universal rules derived from another, albeit more pure, world. On the contrary, they arise in concrete life in the realm of phenomena. Whatever value such rules may have in making moral judgments, in lived life the same rules are not always applicable. No moral judgments are without qualification applicable to all human beings. On the contrary, moral judgments, like the life contexts to which these judgments apply, are always concrete. Abstract laws cannot capture what is right or wrong in any particular context. Good and bad are values that apply to concrete relations between particular conscious subjects, and it is these concrete relations, not abstract rules, that determine the values.

Still, it is not the case that Kant's moral rules are irrelevant. In short, Kant's general rules for moral judgment amount to the following assertion: do not treat others as mere objects; treat them rather as ends in themselves. In knowing an object we know something that we can use. However, it is never right to treat an other—that which is not us—as an object. Hence, even the act of knowing an other is not moral. In general, "not moral" here means morally neutral, non-moral. However, if the other is something like us, that is, another conscious subject, then to reduce the other to an object of our knowledge, even an object of our consciousness, is more than non-moral. With such others there is a duty to treat them as non-objective, as something that is not a thing, as someone whose demands upon us are equal in moral value to our demands upon ourselves, as (in Kant's words) "ends in themselves."

What Buber accepts from this Kantian picture of the domain of the ethical is that morality deals with the domain of will rather than objects, and that others must be treated not as a means to an end but as ends in themselves. He does not accept, however, that these "facts" of morality constitute rules for moral judgments. Rather, there are two ways in which an other can be treated. One way is as a means to an end, as an object or (in Buber's words) as an "it" (Es). Another way is as an end in itself, as another subject like ourselves, as a loved-one, or (in Buber's words) as a "you" in the intimate sense of the term (Du) and not in its impersonal sense (Sie), that is, as a (in now archaic English) "thou."

Hence, contrary to Kant, the domain of the moral is not separable from the domain of the phenomenal. All objects are given to us in experience as something other than ourselves. Whether the object is an object is itself not objective. When the other is experienced as an object, as something that can be differentiated from us as an instrument to serve our will, then it is an it, a thing, and our relationship to it is an "Ich–Es" relationship. Such relationships are the domain of theoretical wisdom, which, as such, are scientific and morally neutral. However, when the same other is experienced as another subject, indistinguishable from ourselves as subjects in no respect other than being other, that is, not being us, then it is a thou, a person, and our relationship to it is an "Ich–Du" relationship. Note that these two relations do not distinguish two kinds of reality. They distinguish two ways in which we as conscious subjects experience reality itself.

From Cohen

Buber's rejection of Kant's radical separation of reality into noumenal and phenomenal realms in itself reflects the influence of the philosophy of Hermann Cohen. A critical separation must be made between the domains of the scientific and the moral. Contrary to the dominant trends in Anglo-American naturalist philosophy, there is and can be no science of ethics. The domain of science is the positivist world of sense objects and their relations. However, the domain of ethics is a radically different world of conscious subjects and the relations between them. In this case the appropriate discipline is religion. Buber accepted that it is religion, not science, to which you look to understand ethics, and the primary subjects of religion—God and his relations to human beings—are intimately tied to ethics.

Kant's God was a noumenal object whose existence was deduced by means of moral arguments. The strategy underlying those arguments was one that said that while we cannot know whether or not God exists, we can know that God ought to exist. As such, God functioned as something ideal rather than actual. Cohen used his model of philosophic thinking based on science's employment of infinite series with finite ends or limits to make Kant's claim intelligible. The phenomenal world is analyzable into sets of processes that are expressible as infinite series directed towards asymptotes, definite limits. These limits are ideals that are more real than the (merely actual) processes that endlessly approximate them. The actual universe itself is also to be understood as such a process, and in this case the end or ideal of all of the universe is God.

However, as Cohen himself recognized,[6] while natural philosophy may be sufficient to know that this deity is real, it is not sufficient to know anything else about him. Most importantly, it is not enough to know what this God wants from his human creatures. For that knowledge, God must reveal himself to them, and the record of that revelation is the content of religion. It is a content that is totally concrete in its nature. It expresses a moral code that can and should guide the life of individual human beings in all of their inter-human relations. It is a code by which we learn values such as compassion (Mitleid) for others, values that are unattainable through philosophy and science alone.[7]

---

[6] Or, at least came to recognize by the end of his career as a philosopher.

[7] In speaking of the kind of (limited) ethics of which philosophy is capable, Cohen argued in *Religion der Vernunft aus den Quellen des Judentums* (English translation, *The Religion of Reason out of the Sources of Judaism*, referred to below as "RV") that (quoting

Buber takes over all of these judgments from Cohen about the interrelationship of natural philosophy/science, religion, and ethics, and develops them further into a dialectic of how to think about all human institutions, not just religion. In doing so, he distinguishes between "religion" as a way of conscious living in interpersonal relationships and "religion" as an institution. As an institution it is no different than any other institution. In all of them there is interpersonal life as well as non-personal existence, and here the institution of religion has no special status. Buber spells out this judgment in his major work in philosophy, *I and Thou*. All institutions reflect God's presence and all of them express alienation from it. As such, all of them are domains for the moral, the immoral, and/or the non-moral. However, it is also true, as both Kant and Cohen assert in their significantly different ways, that theology, religion, and ethics are intimately interconnected and unavoidably associated.

Theology

These claims, then, are Buber's intellectual inheritance, which are presumed, either affirmatively or negatively, in Buber's theology. I will turn now directly to what he says.

The Eternal Thou

For Buber everything, with only one exception, can be expressed as either I–You (Ich–Du) or I–It (Ich–Es). This is not a statement about the way that something is substantially. There are no substances in Buber's philosophy. Things are not independent entities that enter into relationships with other independent entities. Rather, there are only relationships, where substances or things are constructs out of these relations. Everything, again with one exception, is given in both of these relationships. Neither is primary. Everything is both an object for other knowers and a knower who grasps others as objects. Similarly, everything stands in concrete moral relations to others through which they experience and are experienced by others in compassion as lovers as well as loved ones. Knowing is the purest

---

Andrea Poma in *The Critical Philosophy of Hermann Cohen* [English translation by John Denton. Albany: SUNY Press, 1997]) ethics "cannot understand the other man as 'You,' but only as 'He,' not as a *Mitmensch*, but only as a *Nebenmensch* and, being unable to reach the full meaning of the interpersonal relationship, turns out to be unsatisfactory for us as a task... (cf. RV 17f.; Eng. trans. 14f.)... Religion discovers the other man as *Mitmensch* in suffering."

example of an I–It relationship; loving is the purest example of an I–Thou relationship. However, these are only examples.

The exception to this rule is God. God is always experienced in an I–Thou relationship. Hence, contrary to the claims of the philosophers, God knows nothing and is totally unknowable. What God does, exclusively, is love and be loved, and loving is not a cognitive activity. In this sense, at least, Buber follows the rabbinic traditions that, when discussing the God of revelation, tell stories that speak of him on the model of the Song of Songs, which is the central text that they used for commentary in order to express an understanding of revelation. That God reveals himself to Israel means that God loves Israel, and the rabbinic story of the relationship between God and Israel is understood as a love story.

How does Buber interpret this story? He does so as part of a general dialectic of movement through history between these two primary forms of relationship–I–Thou and I–It.

The Dialectic of the Two Ways of Being

Buber's most important work in philosophical theology is *I and Thou*.[8] It begins with a discussion of language. Here he presents the basic concepts of I–Thou and I–It summarized above. What is critical in this format is that it locates Buber clearly within the tradition of modern, western philosophy, where, in direct contrast to both ancient and medieval philosophy, including Jewish philosophy, thinking about the traditional topics of philosophy—God, the world, and the human, that is, the subject matter of metaphysics, physics, psychology and ethics—roots itself in linguistics. Buber begins by saying that the forms of verbs in western languages are hierarchically related such that some forms are logically and linguistically prior to others. The singular is prior to the plural, and the first person is prior to both the second and third. Plurals are constructed from singulars, and the second and third persons as subject forms are derivative from the two ways that objects are related to subjects—personally and impersonally. Personal and impersonal objects are expressed as subjects respectively in the second and third persons. Hence, the central theme of Buber's analysis of language is that through language we experience the world in two forms of relation—I–Thou and I–It.

---

[8] *Ich und Du* (Heidelberg: Lambert Schneider, 1958). English translation by Walter Kaufmann, *I and Thou* (New York: Scribner, 1970).

Buber uses this understanding of language to discuss how we function in social relationships, that is, in relationship to other human beings. The prime example is love between two people, which he characterizes as a three-stage movement—from a pure I–Thou relationship, to a complex relationship where the I–Thou is associated with an I–It (I–Thou/It relation), to a pure I–It relationship.

Associated with the I–Thou is vivacity as well as instability. When the relationship is purely I–Thou, it is intimate and alive. Both the I and the thou give themselves to each other in a way that only living persons can. It is also an ultimate manifestation of love, because each is totally present to the other without any thought of exploitation for the advantage of a self. However, the relation is unstable, because there is no way to guarantee from moment to moment that the relationship will continue.

On Buber's view it is primarily this need for stability, to find ways for the relationship to continue, that initiates the movement of the I–Thou in the direction of becoming I–It. After the initial stage of the relationship, the unknown other becomes associated with identifying marks—a name, a description, a temporal-spatial location, and so on—simply to be able to find the other and to know that the other whom I meet today (i.e., in the present) is the same other whom I met yesterday (i.e., in the past) and will be the same person I can meet tomorrow (i.e., in the future). At this stage the "its" of identity are only tools to meet the person, but in time, as the number of its increases, progressively (or, retrogressively) these identities become who the other is. Then, when the relationship has become pure I–It and the I–Thou is lost, the relationship is held together primarily by usefulness and/or a memory of what was, in the hope that perhaps it can be regained. Sometimes it is regained, which is to say, there is renewal. However, more often it dies, and each person seeks separately for new relationships to replace the one that has died, so that they may regain the life whose loss they mourn. However, once found and life is regained, the need for stability reasserts itself, and the process of deterioration begins anew.

In this way, Buber tells us, social institutions are born and die—from marriages, to businesses, to nation-states, to religions. Marriages end in divorce and often lead to new marriages; businesses go bankrupt and others are reborn; nations corrupt and are rebelled against to form new nations; and religions decay into idolatry, to give way to new religions formed either through schism or through renewal.

Religions decay into idolatry, because those prophets who encounter the pure God who is eternally Thou respond to that encounter by formalizing it in memory as a code of law, a Torah. That code, which is a memorial to the encounter, a way to recapture the encounter, decays into a dogmatic assertion of the will or word of God. At first that written word is associated with the living God, but in time it replaces it. Dogmas—either in the form of statements of purported true beliefs (especially in the case of Christianity) or in the form of imperatives of correct behavior (especially in the case of Judaism)—at first are used as ways to reexperience the initial (prophetic) experiences with God, as a way to be sure that the deity encountered today is the deity who encountered our ancestors in the past as well as a way to secure the continuance of the relationship into the future. However, inevitably the dogmatic form of identity becomes the identity itself.

Buber uses this structure to present a history of Judaism, from its origins in prophecy through multiple schisms that produced Christianity and rabbinic Judaism out of the decay of prophetic religion—Protestantism out of Roman Catholic Christianity, and Hasidism out of a stagnant rabbinic Judaism.[9] For decadent Christianity, God/Christ becomes nothing more than a set of assertions about his nature, so that worship of God/Christ decays into a worship of dogmatic beliefs called catechisms. Similarly, for decadent Judaism, God becomes nothing more than a set of rules that express his will, so that worship of God decays into a worship of dogmatic laws called Torah.

The source of the idolatry is the inescapable need that human beings have for stability, which expresses itself as a wish for certainty, which manifests itself as a desire for knowledge. This need-become-wish-become-desire reaches the level of idolatry when, as in the case of classical Jewish philosophy, the pursuit of knowledge becomes identified with the imitation of God, the attainment of wisdom (theoretical or practical) becomes the highest moral human end (called "happiness"), and this rationalist happiness is identified with God.

However, Buber's God cannot in any sense be grasped. That is his nature. Revelation properly understood is a contentless appearance of God, as nothing more than presence, in the present. It cannot be understood; it has no content other than the awareness that the other who is radically other appeared to you in the concrete, and that you love the other as the other loves you—for you yourself alone and for no purpose whatsoever.

---

[9] Buber does not consider progressive Judaism to be a form of renewal. He does not say explicitly why he does not. I assume it is because of its rationalist faith in the value of human reason as a way to reform belief as well as the rigid formalist structure of its liturgical changes. Far more in keeping with Buber's understanding of revelation would be contemporary Jewish renewal institutions such as P'nai Or.

If I–Thou describes what "good" is, as it did for Kant, the love of God is the ultimate expression of love, and the love of any other human being, any neighbor, is its imitation. However, knowledge is not love. Hence, the classical Jewish philosophers, like their counterparts in Christianity and Islam, were deeply mistaken and seriously misleading to others, when they identified knowledge with revelation and wisdom with God. In truth, revelation yields no knowledge and God has nothing to do with at least this kind of wisdom.

Is the God of Buber Believable?

In my judgment no philosophy is better suited to make intelligible what western liberal religions such as Judaism claim about revelation than Martin Buber's analysis of encounter with God. On this analysis the Hebrew Scriptures are a record of the initial encounter in prophecy of the God whom Israel professes to worship. As such, it testifies to the truth of revelation. However, it is a truth which entails no commitment to dogma of any form, be it belief or practice. To be sure, the Torah states imperatives of behavior that entail dogmas of belief. However, these in themselves are not what God said. In fact God said nothing. Rather, they are honest expressions of what the prophets believed (mistakenly) that they heard God say. They were misled by their hope to transform an essentially transient experience of God's presence into a stable, ongoing, secure relationship. What they said is worthy of our concern, because it is the word of our ancestors who had the supreme good fortune to have encountered God. Those words might even be valuable for at least some of us as we seek to relate to God as well. However, they are more likely to hinder us in our pursuit.

The experience of God is an experience of pure love. Because of its purity there is no way for it to be invoked at will. To be loved by God is to be chosen by God, and God will choose whom he will choose when he chooses them. Hence, there is no way to guarantee divine presence. All we can do is prepare ourselves to receive it if and when it comes. We do that by loving our fellow human beings, our neighbors. We can identify a neighbor, because neighbors are not only I–Thou. In this sense they are easier to love than God, because they are more like us than God. However, they are not God. They are only a "glimpse" of God. To love them is not the same as loving God; still, it does sensitize us to God and it does prepare us to accept God's love, which otherwise we might pass by without notice. Hence, the closest thing to a dogma that Buber will affirm is that man is created in the image of God (for both enter into I–Thou relations), and his only commandment is to love one's neighbor (for the love of neighbor is both a preparation for and a consequence of the love of God).

All that being said (about how well suited Buber's theology is to liberal religions), it may not be the case that Buber's religious thought is best suited for a theology of Judaism as such. Most critically, it is significant that while Buber speaks about the God of revelation, he says nothing about the God of creation. He cannot, in part because the tendency in the religious philosophy of his time was to divorce religious thought from questions that deal with physical reality, to leave the latter exclusively to the domain of science, and to grant that questions about the origin of the universe are questions about physical reality. Buber is a phenomenologist, which is to say a thinker who limits the domain of his speculation to what can be deduced about reality from what we as human beings can experience, and the origin of the universe in general does not fall within this domain.

It may also be the case that he, following the dominant trends of the science of his day, believed that the universe is eternal and therefore uncreated. In doing so, he was not unusual. Whereas discussions of God in classical Jewish philosophy rooted themselves in thought about God as the creator, and only then extended to thought about God the revealer and the redeemer, almost no Jewish philosopher, from at least the time of Spinoza to the present, dealt with creation. However, if this is the case, Buber's (hypothetical) rejection of the dogma of creation will undermine the very foundations of his theology, for Buber, no less than earlier Jewish theologians, must ground his account of revelation in a theory of creation.

As we saw at the beginning of this discussion of Buber's religious thought, his primary notion that God is an eternal I–Thou—meaning that God is radically unlike anything else that exists in that he can in no way be subject to objectification, especially as an object of knowledge—is drawn from Maimonides' negative theology, but the basis of that theology is Maimonides' analysis of what it means to say that God is the creator and everything else is a creature. If there is no creation, God cannot be a creator, and if God is not a creator, there is no radical separation between God and everything else in the way that Buber claims there to be.

The absence of any association of the God of revelation with the God of creation in Buber's theology is unacceptable for yet another reason. A revealer deity who is not the creator is inadequate as the God of Judaism even if he be affirmed to be the revealer of the Torah, for creation is no less (possibly more) a root-principle (*'iqqar*) of Judaism than is revelation. Furthermore, even if it were the case that the universe is temporally eternal (which is not obviously the case on the authority of physics alone; at least our universe is considered by almost all scientists today to have a definite point of origin in time), that would not mean that it was not created by God, since almost without exception the classical Jewish philosophers considered creation to express a non-temporal activity. Hence, on at least these grounds—that Buber's God of revelation is not the God of creation—Buber's theology is unsatisfactory for present purposes.

However, this is not its only weakness. It is more critical that while Buber makes intelligible the notion of a God who can reveal himself to human beings, including Moses, what this view of revelation says about the Torah is problematic. While Buber does not reject the Torah as such, his radically antinomian interpretation of it does mean that any claim that the Torah makes proper demands upon us, both for belief and practice, is worse than wrong—it is inherently idolatrous. The liberal Judaism that follows, therefore, from Buber's theology is a Judaism in which all that matters is personal relations between people. Nothing else can be required or even sanctioned. This liberal Judaism is a viable form of Jewish religion, but on Buber's terms such a religion is inherently imperialist, because it entails the illegitimacy of every other form of Judaism—especially Orthodoxy. For most religiously affirmative Jews, the Torah and rabbinic tradition are not idolatrous. That tradition makes legitimate claims on both our beliefs and our practices, and the authority for that legitimacy is that the Torah at least is in some significant sense revealed. If this account is correct, Buber's conception of the God of revelation and his revelation cannot be true.

Where, then, can we turn to find a theology of revelation and the revealer that both affirms the authoritative legitimacy of the Torah and rabbinic tradition and leaves room for individual judgment about what in it is compelling, that is, true and right? It is with this question in mind that I turn to the theology of Buber's close colleague and friend, Franz Rosenzweig.

THE CONCEPT OF 'NICHTS' IN ROSENZWEIG'S "STAR OF REDEMPTION"

Norbert M. Samuelson

I am in the beginning stages of researching a book on the history of the concept בראשית ברא אלהים in Jewish philosophy. The most important modern Jewish philosopher to deal with this עקר was Franz Rosenzweig. This paper is one small part of this planned study. Rosenzweig interpreted בראשית ברא אלהים to mean, in some sense, *creatio ex nihilo*. This paper deals with what Rosenzweig meant by *ex nihilo* in this context.

The primary text where Rosenzweig discusses his doctrine of creation is Part II, Book 1 of *Der Stern der Erlösung*.[1] However, that discussion presupposes what Rosenzweig already said about the concept of *Nichts* (= *nihil* = nothing) in Part I. Primarily because of time limitations, this paper is further restricted to what Rosenzweig says about *Nichts* in Part I of *The Star*.

Introduction: The New Philosophy

Rosenzweig's introduction consists of preparatory remarks on the movement from Hegel's philosophy of the All to a new philosophy based on three nothings of knowledge, viz., the nothing of knowledge of man, the world, and God. He tells us that when philosophy rejected death as something (*Etwas*, by which he means something posited), it turned death into a nothing (*Nichts*) that stands outside of the domain of philosophy, and he identified philosophy's subject-matter with *Sein*, which Rosenzweig equates with Hegel's *All*. (*Star*, 7–9/3–6) Furthermore, Rosenzweig implies that the All also is the general. On Rosenzweig's analysis there is a sharp contrast between *Sein* or *the All* or what is general on one hand, and

---

This chapter was first published in *The New Thinking and its Dimensions, Volume II*, by Wolf Dietrich-Smith Kowarzik, Freiburg: Verlag Karl Alber (1988): 643–656. Reprinted with permission.

[1] *The Star of Redemption*, henceforth to be referred to as *Star*. All page references will be to the German edition, Heidelberg: Lambert Schneider 1954, and William Hallo's English translation, Boston: Beacon Press 1972, in such a way that "n/m" means page n of the German edition and page m of the English translation.

nothing or the individual on the other hand. In other words, in the very opening sections of Rosenzweig's introduction (*Star*, 7–12/3–7) it already is clear that whatever else he means by *Nichts*, it is individual rather than general, it stands outside of what philosophic reasoning can encompass even though it is real, and its opposites are *Sein* and *Etwas*.

The *Nichts* of knowledge of man marks the transcendence of ethics and the beginning of metaethics. (*Star*, 16–17/10–11) Ethics deals with world view (*Weltanschauung*). It concentrates on human actions expressed in the formation of commands, and its subject-matter is a view of man in general. In contrast, metaethics deals with life-view (*Lebensanschauung*). It concentrates on man as something that is passive who receives rather than initiates commands, and its subject matter is a view of man as individual.

The *Nichts* of knowledge of world marks the transcendence of logic and the beginning of metalogic. (*Star*, 19–22/12–15) This transcendence is based on the logical claim that the domain of reason does not include everything that is real. Rosenzweig offers two arguments for this judgment. (*Star*, 19–20/12–13) For our purpose, only the first argument is important. Reason is a process of defining. It consists in stipulating a genus and a specification, or, in Rosenzweig's words, stating that something is such (the genus) and not otherwise (the specific difference). Whereas the first activity unifies being, the second separates. Consequently, the very way that reason operates entails that what is one in being is diverse in thought. Consequently, there is more to reality than can be grasped by philosophy.

This separation of reason and being entails a separation between logic and metalogic. Logic deals with the world in general. Through expressing laws of necessity it unifies thought about reality, but logic does not unify reality. In contrast, metalogic deals with the concrete world of individuals. By expressing contingency rather than necessity, and content rather than laws, metalogic and metalogic alone can unify the reality of the world.

The *Nichts* of knowledge of God is the transcendence of physics and the beginning of metaphysics. (*Star*, 24–28/16–19) As man as an individual is beyond the generalizations of ethics and the individuality of the world is beyond the university of the world, so God as an individual is beyond what can be known through philosophy as God. Furthermore, since the subject-matter of each meta-x is beyond the domain of x, and the domain of physics is being, the God revealed through metaphysics is beyond being. Based on the development of this insight from Schelling through Nietzsche (*Star*, 26–27/18), Rosenzweig concludes that as man is beyond his nature (being) in having will, and the world is beyond its nature by being created, so God is beyond his nature by being free.

We have already noted that for Rosenzweig the *Nichts* stands in opposition to *Sein* and *Etwas*. Furthermore, whatever *Nichts* is, it deals with what is individual rather than what is general. In the case of man, individuality refers to his life and will. In the case of God, individuality expresses His freedom, and in case of the world, individuality involves its concrete, contingent content. In contrast, the world of *Sein* is a world of natures that reason comprehends through laws and definitions that express what is both universal and necessary. In other words reality is composed of a series of opposites—nothing and being, individuals and universals, contingency and necessity—in each case philosophic reasoning can only comprehend the latter, and only by understanding both can we come to terms with all of reality. Being is the subject-matter of the form of reasoning appropriate to philosophy. Beyond philosophy is metaphilosophy, whose subject-matter is *Nichts*.

If we concentrate our attention solely on the element world, we cannot help but notice the similarity between Rosenzweig's and Aristotle's ontologies. For Aristotle, as for Rosenzweig, the real world is composed of two radically different principles—matter (*hyle*) and form (*morphe*). The former is what accounts for the individual, contingent, concrete content, while the latter expresses general natures. Similarly, being (*ousia*) belongs to the world of forms that constitute the subject matter that philosophy expresses through necessary definitions and universal laws, while privation stands on the edge of intelligibility in Aristotle's science pointing to a reality of concrete chance happenings that lie beyond philosophical reason's grasp. Rosenzweig's analysis of the element man can also fit into an Aristotelian model where acts of will are acknowledged insofar as ethics apply only to what is voluntary, but willing itself stands outside of Aristotle's stipulation of the laws governing moral acts. Any attempt to apply what Rosenzweig says about God in this case to Aristotle's theology is more problematic, but here the difficulty has nothing to do with their respective use of the term, nothing. Rather, the issue is their understanding of God, for Rosenzweig's deity is subject to negation while Aristotle's is not.[2]

---

[2] I do not mean to suggest that Rosenzweig adopted Aristotle's ontology. On the contrary, from what he says in several passages in *The Star* (e.g., *Star*, 71–72/53–54), it seems clear to me that Rosenzweig rejected what he thought was Aristotle's ontology, but he misunderstood Aristotle. Furthermore, in spite of his error, he adopted an Aristotelian ontology that he did not realize was Aristotelian. However, a proof of this claim lies beyond the confines of this paper, since it would require an entire article in its own right. Let it suffice for our purpose to point out the similarity between the ontologies of Aristotle and Rosenzweig, and leave open any questions of historical influence.

The introduction begins with Hegel's philosophy (*Star*, 9 ff./5 ff.) and concludes with Rosenzweig's new philosophy (*Star*, 12 ff./7 ff.). From Hegelian rational sciences of theology, cosmology and psychology and their corresponding elements God, world and man, we move by way of negation to Rosenzweig's meta-rational sciences. Hegel's sciences posit something (an *Etwas*), the negation of which yields three distinct instances of nothing (*Nichts*) that are the starting point of Rosenzweig's analysis. Rosenzweig calls them "irrational" objects" (*Star*, 28/19). However, as we see in the body of Part I, "irrational" should not be understood to mean incomprehensible. They are no more and no less intelligible than are irrational numbers in mathematics. Rather, just as a new math was required to encompass irrational as well as rational numbers, so Rosenzweig begins a new philosophy to encompass the irrational as well as the rational elements of reality.

At this stage all that we know about these objects is that we know nothing about them. However, our interest here is not with spelling out Rosenzweig's new philosophy, but exploring what Rosenzweig at this stage of development tells us about *Etwas*, the rational object of philosophy, and *Nichts*, the irrational object of his new philosophy. Rosenzweig's goal in Part I of the Star is to start with something concrete, through analysis to negate it as known, and then to posit or affirm it as something that otherwise is unknown. The *Nichts* is what is negated as known, and the *Etwas* at the beginning of Part II is what is posited or affirmed from what had been negated. The *Etwas* is something indefinite. It is, but it is undefined. In other words, it is what in ordinary modern logic would be called a variable. In contrast, the initial *Nichts* in all three meta-sciences are definite nothings. In each case meta-scientists begin with something concrete that is subsequently negated. They are not just nothing; they are the nothing of what was negated. In other words, Rosenzweig's *Nichts* in the new philosophy occupies a place similar to if not identical with Aristotle's understanding of privation, in clear opposition to what otherwise might be called absolute nothing.[3]

The introduction concludes with a discussion of Hermann Cohen's infinitesimal calculus. (*Star*, 29–32/20–22) It is here that Rosenzweig makes explicit his ontology of something and nothing. Rosenzweig explicitly claims that this calculus provided him with a model for constructing reality from what is practically (but not absolutely) nothing. As the old

---

[3] Again, no claim is made that Rosenzweig understood what he was doing in these Aristotelian terms.

philosophy began with pure form (à la Aristotle), so the new philosophy begins with pure matter (again, à la Aristotle). The something that follows from Rosenzweig's negation of nothing is not something positive (i.e., it is not an Aristotelian form or being). Whatever the similarities in ontology, Rosenzweig's philosophy is really a new philosophy. Rather, what follows is something that is still negative. It is the negation of what is negative. As such it is something that falls under what Kant called an "infinite judgment". In all three new sciences—the distinct moves from the *Nichts* to the *Etwas* of God, man and world respectively—what emerges are "elements" of reality. These elements are three relative nothings modeled on a wedding of Kant's infinite judgment and Cohen's infinitesimal calculus. In other words, as it becomes spelled out in greater detail in the body of Part I, the *Nichts* of the creation of Part II Book 1 is a construct understood on the mathematical model of the infinitesimal.

Book One: God and Metaphysics

What we deduced about the *Nichts* in relation to the *Etwas* in the introduction becomes explicit in Rosenzweig's discussion of negative theology in the opening sections of Book 1. There he spells out his methodology. (*Star*, 34–36/24–26) Traditional theology went from *Etwas* to *Nichts*. It began with positive claims about God and ended in Maimonides' negative theology. (*Star*, 33–34/23) In contrast, Rosenzweig's metaphysics moves from the *Nichts* to the *Etwas* of God's reality (*Wirklichkeit*). In reaching this end the new philosophy follows two compatible methods. (*Star*, 34/24) First, as we saw in the introduction, it examines its beginning (*Anfang*) and negates it. The beginning as a beginning is something finite and definite, but because it is negated it is an act (*Tat*) of liberation. Second, as emerges in the books of Part I, Rosenzweig's new philosophy inquires into and affirms its point of departure (*Ursprung*) as a double negation, a "*Nichtnichts*". Because this origin is affirmed it is a being (*Wesen*), but because it is a double negation it is something infinite.

Rosenzweig introduces his model meta-scientific sentence and describes its logical mode. (*Star*, 38–39/27–28) In a sentence of the form "$y = x$", the left hand term is the grammatical subject, the semantic subject and a negative supposition (*Setzung*). Conversely, the right hand term is the grammatical predicate, the semantic content, and an affirmative determination of the subject (*Bestimmung*). In Rosenzweig's logic, a sentence of this form expresses a universal conditional (If anything is a y then it is a x.) and not an identity claim.

Rosenzweig's metaphysics affirms in his symbolic language, "A = A". (*Star*, 39–46/28–33) The "A" of the left-hand place is the point of departure. It is the *Nichts* of any knowledge of God from the conclusion of Maimonides' theology. Rosenzweig calls it divine freedom (*Freiheit*) because, lacking any content, it entails no limitation on God. (*Star*, 39–42/28–30)

At this stage Rosenzweig posits of God the oneness that Maimonides affirmed. God and God alone is nothing of which anyone can think. The left-hand "A" is an act of affirmation of a negated essence. In more traditional terms, it is the act of negating of God everything that is finite. Conversely, the "= A" is an act of negating an infinite number of somethings any of which would limit God if they could be affirmed of Him, precisely because they are something (*Etwas*). (*Star*, 42–43/30–31) In other words, God is free because nothing can be affirmed of him. He is free from every limitation. He is infinitely free, because there are an infinite number of things that He is not; and He is eternally free, because nothing that will ever come to be will be God. Consequently, God as God is continuously not what He creates.

This way of not being something also expresses God's nature. In this sense, the right-hand "A" is called divine essence (*Wesen*). (*Star*, 42–43/30–31) It is an asymptopic movement of divine freedom towards the idea of divine essence. The freedom is a force with a direction, whereas the essence simply is and therefore has no direction. The freedom is a potentiality, whereas an essence is an actuality. It is this movement that "A = A" expresses. God's original infinite freedom becomes increasingly constrained and transformed into divine power and caprice, while the divine essence is transformed into divine fate and obligation. Through the endless passage of time in which an unceasing number of somethings are created, the more divine freedom (God as subject) becomes his essence (God is content). As such "A = A" is a statement that can only be understood in terms of Cohen's calculus. The sentence expresses an equation for the activity of creation which, when diagrammed, has a particular nothing as its starting point and constantly approximates but never reaches an end point or limit that is 1.

For the purposes of this paper, what is most important to note about the above summary, is that in any meta-scientific sentence, whose logical form is "y = x", the sentence expresses a function that begins from a starting point that is nothing and moves towards an end point that is something. In the case of metaphysics, God is expressed by the equation "A = A" which states the function of creation, the left-hand "A" is the nothing from which creation takes place, and this nothing is God's nature as subject. It is that particular nothing which can be characterized as divine freedom. It is the affirmation that whatever it is it is not God.

In this context, "*creatio ex nihilo*" expresses that the relative nothing of the knowledge of God (the "*ex nihilo*") is the origin from which God acts to become God (the "*creatio*"). The *nihil* is divine freedom. It is a negative supposition that whatever is or will be is not God. The *creatio* is the equal sign of the equation "A = A". The equation expresses a function in infinitesimal calculus. The equation itself is creation from the perspective of metaphysics.

Book Two: The World and Metalogic

The somethings that are not God that God creates are the content of the world. Creation expresses a relation between God and world. In God's case, creation is the function expressed in the equation (A = A) that is God. In the world's case, creation is the function expressed in the equation (B = A) that is the world becoming God.[4]

The subject-matter of metalogic is the conclusion of negative cosmology. It is all that remains of the world that is self-evident when God or man are made the point of departure. In Rosenzweig's reading of the history of philosophy that remainder is the *Ding an sich*, which he characterizes as an "infinitesimal residue".[5] As in the case of the element God, where by affirming the infinite judgment (*das Nichtnichts*) we affirmed the infinite essence of God, so in the case of the element world, we affirm an infinite judgment. However, in this case what is affirmed is a Logos rather than an essence. The Logos is world reasoning (*Denken*). (*Star*, 57/43) This reasoning is an abstract hypothetical whose validity is demonstrated through its universal, and therefore necessary, application to absolutely every something (*Etwas*) in the world. As such it is an *a priori*, abstract hypothetical. Therefore, it itself is not in the world. Conceqently, the essence (*Wesen*) of the world (*Logos*) is something that itself is neither the world nor in the world. This essence is what Rosenzweig expressed in his symbolic language about the element God as "= A" (*Star*, 59/44).

The Logos of the world has the logical status of the "x" in "given any x, if x is A then x is B" that is the standard way of expressing in contemporary logic "All A is B". The "A" of Rosenzweig's "= A" asserts universal applicability *qua* applicability, independent of any content. The equal sign in this equation expresses the potentiality of this A (Logos) to be applied to absolutely

---

[4] Compare *Star*, 66/50, with *Star*, 86/65.
[5] *Star*, 55/41: "unendlich kleiner Restbetrag"/"infinitesimal residuum".

every something in the world. In other words, "= A" expresses a potentiality for infinite creativity out of the specific *Nichts* of the world. This capacity is independent of any order or intelligibility of any spiritual creativity that might be applied to the world from without. As such, again, independent of anything else, the world in itself endlessly creates its parts. These parts, that are neither observed nor understood, constitute the world's plenitude (*Fülle*). (*Star*, 60/45) They are a kind of product (*Gebilde*)[6] that is constantly renewed (*erneuert*) out of the world's *Nichts*. (*Star*, 60/45) This *Nichts* generates endlessly an infinite number of original, concrete particulars, each of which is uniquely itself and devoid of any ordering or inherent intelligibility.

Each one of the infinite number of world-particulars is in itself a specific nothing. They are each meaningless, but they are not generally meaningless. Each is singularly nothing and uniquely meaningless. Each nothing is a nothing of its own something. The being that each lacks is its own being that makes it its own something. Similarly, each lacks its own meaning and intelligibility. In Rosenzweig's language, each is a "not-otherwise."[7] His symbol to express this individuality is "B". (*Star*, 61/46) B is contrary to order and intelligibility. It is complete, absolute individuality. It is "Not-Otherwiseness" (*Besonderheit*).

Rosenzweig's equation for the world is "B = A". (*Star*, 66–68/50–51) B is a total distinctiveness that constitutes the complete, absolute individuality of everything that becomes real in the world. It is the act of negation (*das Nein*) of the *Nichts* of the world which, when conjoined to God's act of affirmation (*das Ja*), "God's Physis", gives rise to each "individual (*Einzelnes*) something (*Etwas*)". (*Star*, 62–66/46–50) God's Physis is expressed in the equation of the world as "A". In this logical syntax, the nature of God becomes the universal (*das Allgemeine*). The equal sign expresses their conjunction (*das Und*). The individuals of the world are produced by an endless process of interaction between the particular (B) and the universal (A). Each side of the equation is incomplete without the other. The universal is passive. It simply is, and as such it needs application. This need generates a force of attraction (*eine anziehende Kraft*) upon the particular, which, because it is aimless, is drawn to the universal.

In the process that is the world, whose equation is "B = A", the B becomes conscious that it is being attracted towards the A, and thereby is transformed from a mere particular (*Besonderes*) into an individual (*Individuum*). (*Star*,

---

[6] Hallo calls it "creation". I would prefer to reserve this term for *Schöpfung*.
[7] "*Nicht-anders*", *Star*, 60/45.

64/47–48) An individual is a meaningless, totally unique creature who becomes conscious that it no longer is aimless and increasingly becomes dominated by a universal. To the extent, but only to the extent, that the individual is dominated by its universal, it becomes its species (*Gattung*). (*Star*, 64/48) As the particular is not the same as the individual, so the species is not the same as the universal. Species is not just a universal. It is a particular or individuated universal or universality. Its individuality is its freedom, and its universality is its essence. In this conjunction the individual is related to God, whose nature gives it direction and meaning.

Life begins in conception as a distinct nothing with the freedom of infinite possibilities at the cost of total meaninglessness. Life consists of individual movement in the direction of God's nature. This motion gives life meaning at the cost of freedom. As the individual continuously approaches this infinitely distant limit, it increasingly becomes its species (*Gattung*), which, in final fulfillment, would be identical with "world essence". As such the equation "B = A" expresses the process of life. "B" is the *Besondere*. It is the content of the world that includes every particular as particular. "A" is the *Allgemeine*. It is the passive form of the world that includes every form and order of the world as form and order. The equal sign expresses a non-reversible relation between A and B in which B is continuously attracted to A. "B = A" states that B penetrates and fills A.

We already noted in connection with the introduction to Part One, that Rosenzweig's implicit ontology is remarkably Aristotelian. At this point the resemblance between their respective theories of physics should also be apparent. Rosenzweig's world is composed of individual somethings, each of which is a conjunction of an universal species (*Gattung*) and an utterly distinct particular that in itself lacks order and meaning (*Besonderes*). The distinct particular component accounts for the existence of the individual, while the species gives it meaning. The meaning is teleological. Every individual life consists of a directed motion whose object is its species, and that species ultimately is an expression of what is simultaneously God's nature and the world's essence.

The terms *Gattung, Besonderes* and *Individuum* function in Rosenzweig's metalogic in the same way that the corresponding terms form (*morphe*), matter (*hyle*) and individual substance (*ousia*) function in Aristotle's physics. Note that Rosenzweig's *Nichts*, like Aristotle's *hyle*, is not absolutely nothing. Both terms name a principle of individuality, contingency, and potentiality that reason needs and points to but cannot as reason encompass. Rosenzweig's *Nichts*, like Aristotle's *hyle*, is a fundamental principle by which the concrete world of material entities is comprehended. That intelligibility is expressed through a relationship in which Being (*Sein*) constitutes the opposite pole.

In Rosenzweig's language, the world is expressed as B = A, which means that what is a *Besonderes* is attracted to what is an *Allgemeines*. The All or the universal is the pole of being; the distinctive or the particular is the pole of nothing. Rosenzweig's nothing is a relative, concrete nothing that actively becomes Rosenzweig's something. That something ultimately is expressed as the limit of an equation in Cohen's version of the infinitesimal calculus. Being is the limit of that equation. It is Rosenzweig's absolute, universal something that passively attracts Rosenzweig's noting. In other words, nothing is the opposite of something and functions as the point of departure in an equation whose end or limit is absolutely something. That equation expresses the world of individuals through all time in terms of a life process that Rosenzweig identifies with creation.

Book Three: Man and Metaethics

As Maimonides' negative theology in the middle ages introduced the doubt about God, and Descartes' reflections at the beginning of the modern period introduced doubt about the world (*Star*, 56/42), so Kant's Transcendental Unity of Apperception at the beginning of the contemporary period introduces doubt about man. (*Star*, 82–83, 88/62–63, 67) Each doubt provides the distinct *Nichts* that begins the corresponding new sciences of metaphysics, metalogic and metaethics. As the initial doubt about God yielded the *Ja* of the creating (*schaffende*) nature or physis of God ("A"), and from our initial doubt of the world arose the *Nein* of the generating (*zeugende*) of particularity ("B"), and the conjunction (*Und*) of the two resulted in the ordering (*Gestalt*) of the individual (*Individuum*), so in this case from our initial doubt of man we move to a *new Ja, Nein* and *Und* with appropriate symbols. (*Star*, 83/63)

As it is the essence of God to be immortal and it is the essence of the world to be necessary, it is the essence (*Wesen*) of man to be transitory (*vergänglich*). (*Star*, 84/63) Similarly, as the existence of God is to be unconditional and the existence of the world is to be universal, the existence (*Sein*) of man is to be distinctive (*Besonderes*). The affirmation (*Ja*) of man's essence yields his essence as an infinite judgment (a *Nichtnichts*). His essence is a contentless-yet-affirmative precondition for knowledge about or in the world through which, in every act of knowing, man knows himself as something there (*da*) and distinct (*besonders*) from the very act through which this essence is revealed. (*Star*, 84/64) As such, man knows himself to be so distinctive that he can recognize no other uniqueness but his own. It is this perception of radical distinctiveness (*Besonderheit*) that is the root-affirmation (*Urja*) of his essence. (*Star*, 85/64–65) Rosenzweig calls it man's idiosyncracy (*Eigenheit*). (*Star*, 83/63) This idiosyncracy constitutes man's "character" (*Star*, 85/65). It individuates man in every one of his actions. Its symbol is "B" (*Star*, 86/65). In the context of metaethics, "B" is man's singularity (*Eigenheit*). With respect to metalogic, it is an affirmation (*Ja*) of his particularity (*Besonderheit*).

The B of man's limited existence is related as the direct contrary of the A of God's infinite existence. (*Star*, 86/65–66) While B stands in some kind of relation to A in metaethics, it is in no way like the "= A" relation of metaphysics and metalogic. B's relation to A is so dissimilar to "= A" that it could be expressed (although Rosenzweig does not do so) by the equation "B = A". (*Star*, 86–88/66–67) "B = A" says that the relation (*Beziehung*) between B and A is that there is no relation. (*Star*, 90/68)

That man and world have the same symbol, B, indicates the relationship between these two elements in Rosenzweig's symbolic language. In the case of the world, B is the *Nein* that expresses the world's particularity. In the case of man, B is the *Ja* which expresses man's permanent character. That character is the freedom (*Freiheit*) of the human will. It is an affirmation (*Ja*) that arises from the infinite judgment (*Nichtnichts*) of the initial doubt of man. Man's freedom differs from God's in that the former is finite and the latter is infinite. In Rosenzweig's symbolism, whereas "A =" expresses God's unlimited freedom to act, which, because it is unlimited, is God's power, in contrast, "B =" expresses man's limited freedom to will, which, because it is limited, is distinct from action and power. As such human free will is a purely intentional or directional kind of act that lacks content or overt expression.

According to Rosenzweig's metaethics, man's free will (B =) becomes conscious of itself as being both finite and unconditional. As such Rosenzweig calls it "defiant will" (*trotziger Wille*). (*Star*, 88–90/67–69) It is the counterpart of God's power. Its determination (*Bestimmung*) is its content. That content is man's character, and that character forms man into a "self". (*Star*, 89/68) Self is the conjunction (*Und*) of defiant will and character. The resulting sum is "the living person" (*der lebendige Mensch*) (*Star*, 88/67). Rosenzweig's equation for this sum is "B = B" (*Star*, 90–92/69–70). The left-hand "B" is man's free will. The right-hand "B" is man's character.

"= B" expresses man's character, which is his singularity (*Eigenheit*) among the world's individuals as that individual who, like God, freely wills. "B =" expresses the defiance of his will, which is conscious that, unlike God, man's will has limitations. "B = B" conjoins the two as self.

"B = B" in metaethics has the same form but not the same content of "B = A" in metalogic. "B = A" expresses how each particular nothing in the world is becoming something universal that is simultaneously God's nature and the content of the world. As such "B = A" is a relational equation. In contrast, "B = B" expresses how the particular something of man is becoming character, which is a nothing. The self that is expressed by "B = B" becomes itself independent of any relation to another self or an universal.

Man as self (B = B) is free will becoming character. It is like the (A = A) of God's divine freedom becoming divine essence in that both equations express a self-contained freedom. However, the freedom in man's case is finite and self-contained, whereas God's freedom is infinite. Similarly, it is like the (B = A) of the world's creation in that it is an equation about what is a finite particularity. However, the particularity of the left-hand "B" in (B = B) is a non-relational self. The equation "B = A" in metaethics expresses human personality. As a personality man is an individual among individuals in the world. As such man is defined by his relationship to other individuals and universals.

Conclusion

The concern in this paper was with Rosenzweig's concept of *Nichts*. That concept is developed in Part I and plays a critical role in developing Rosenzweig's doctrine of creation in Book 1 of Part II. In Rosenzweig's "Transition" (*Übergang*) section at the end of Part I (*Star*, 109–118/83–90) he tells us that at this stage we have only dealt with possibilities for knowledge and not certainties, because we have not as yet moved beyond the actuality (*Tatsächlichkeit*) of the isolated, hypothetical elements of reality to their structure in relationship. The elements emerged and developed in the process of a movement of thought from the *Nichts* of knowledge (*Wissen*) to the *Etwas* of knowledge prior to any visible reality. Part of understanding visible reality will be understanding the relationship of creation that holds between the elements, God and world. That relationship will connect the *Etwas* of God as unlimited power, that emerged out of the *Nichts* of God as infinite freedom, with the *Etwas* of the world as *Gattung*, that functions

THE CONCEPT OF 'NICHTS' IN ROSENZWEIG'S "STAR OF REDEMPTION"   79

as the limit of the directional motion of man and other particulars out of the *Nichts* of their birth as what is utterly unique (*besonders*). Knowledge of the relational movement of creation (*Schöpfung*), as well as of revelation (*Offenbarung*), is knowledge of reality.[8] God, man and world are in themselves only elements, and, as such, are proto-real, i.e., more hypothetical.

At this stage we can say the following about the nothing out of which God creates the world. Creation itself is a non-temporal relation that holds between God and world. It is a relation that is expressed in logical symbolism as a function whose equation is modeled on calculus. That equation is geometrically mapped in two-dimensional space. One dimension is God, and the other is the world. The function is an asymptote, whose starting-point in Cartesian coordinates is (0,0), and whose end point is (1,1) The "1" in both cases is their essence, which, as an ultimate limit, is simultaneously God's oneness, God's power, the world's unity, and the world's content. The 0 in each case is the *Nichts*. Like an infinitesimal, it is a relative nothing out of which everything positive arises.

Together with the *Sein* of philosophy, *Nichts* is the fundamental principle of Rosenzweig's new thinking. In contrast to *Sein*, it is particular rather than general, contingent rather than necessary, and active rather than passive. If it were not for nothing there would only be static, eternal concepts. With

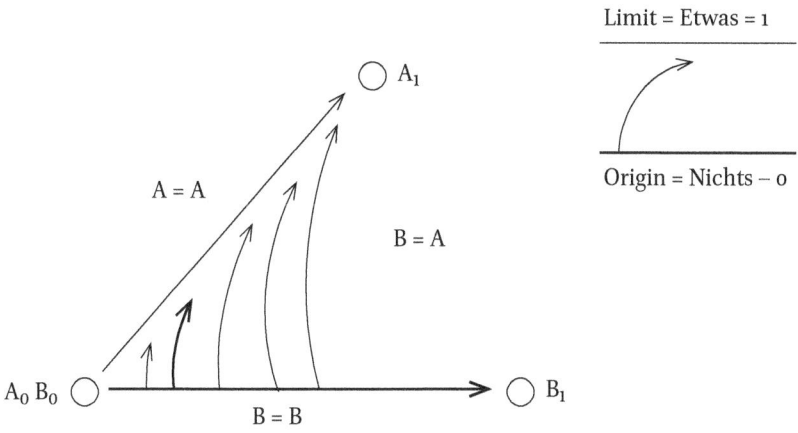

---

[8] *Star*, 118/90. It is important to note that at this stage of Rosenzweig's thinking no reference is made to redemption (*Erlösung*).

nothing there is a vital world of concrete living entities that change and have options, move and are free.

We have already noted in relation to Aristotle that the new thinking is not as new as Rosenzweig thought it was. However, from the perspective of the world of early twentieth century Germany that saw all of philosophy in Hegelian terms, Rosenzweig's Star shines bright as a radical departure in human knowledge. It turns philosophy and science away from the static abstract logic of *Sein* to the dynamic, concrete metalogic of *Nichts*. As Aristotle and the Aristotelians had recognized before philosophy changed with Descartes and the Cartesians, reality is more than what is. What remains is practically nothing at all, but it is the comprehension of that nothing that holds the key to knowing the stars and recognizing redemption.

THE CHALLENGES OF THE MODERN SCIENCES FOR JEWISH FAITH

Norbert M. Samuelson

A. *The Problem*

The Hebrew Scriptures present written evidence for what constitutes at least the intellectual content of the culture of those early Jewish people who were the immediate precursors of Rabbinic Jewish civilization. Of course, this civilization did not come into being out of nothing. It has historical, intellectual, and cultural precursors out of which it developed. Solely for the sake of simplification, we begin with this collection of texts as a complete document irrespective of when this codification takes place. Whenever that occurred, the Hebrew Bible describes in broad and usually general terms what were the accepted, maybe even canonical, beliefs of those Judeans who recognized that the new civilization of (for a word) Hellenism was gaining (or possibly already had gained) hegemony over their biblical, Hebrew civilization. Those Judeans recognized that Hellenistic culture contained challenges to biblical culture that, if allowed to pass without address, threatened to destroy Judea, not by physical force but intellectual domination. In this case the challenge was not primarily from armies but from the persuasiveness of Greco-Roman understandings of the nature of the cosmos and everything in it.

The collected texts of at least the *Tannaim* express the attempt of these earliest rabbis to construct a new understanding of the Hebrew Scriptures. This new understanding would enable a reconstructed form of biblical faith to make sense out of all the postbiblical changes in history, nature, and in thought about history and nature. These changes in themselves threatened the credibility of the faith put forward by the authors and/or editors of the Hebrew Scriptures. In a word, this is how I understand the significance of the development of Rabbinic philosophy in the corpus of

---

"The Challeneges of the Modern Sciences for Jewish Faith" from *CCAR Journal: The Reform Jewish Quarterly*, Winter 2012 © 2012 by Central Conference of American Rabbis and reprinted for use with permission of the CCAR. All rights reserved.

at least tannaitic texts in what had become for subsequent generations of Jews canonical expressions of Jewish faith.

I am not interested in debating here whether or not it is correct to call early Rabbinic writings "philosophy." Certainly it has minimal resemblance to the kind of writings that today, especially in the world of English-language speakers and thinkers, are called "philosophy." However, what British and American academic departments call "philosophy" is not the only understanding of the term. In even this Eurocentric subdivision of Western civilization, it has not been the dominant understanding of what is philosophy, and possibly (in my case I can say hopefully) will not continue to be the dominant understanding of what is philosophy for much longer. For me "philosophy" includes all attempts to make sense out of everything in the most general terms, especially to make sense out of how we human beings locate ourselves in the universe relative to everything else in it. This usage minimally includes other human beings and life forms with whom we interact, all of our physical surroundings both on this planet and in the cosmos, and the entire history of everything insofar as we can understand it, from its temporal or atemporal origins if it has any to its temporal or atemporal ends (again) if it has any.

On this very broad definition of "philosophy" there is nothing special about Jewish philosophy except the specificity of the subject term in its description. Jewish philosophy differs in principle from general philosophy only in the range of the term "we" in the above description. Jewish philosophers in this context attempt to "make sense out of how we" Jews (rather than "human beings" in general) "locate ourselves in the universe relative to everything else in it." Only the subject term in Jewish philosophy is more restricted than the subject term in general philosophy. The rest of the sentence, including the grammatical object related to the grammatical subject, is the same. Jewish philosophy is not reflection solely on the Jewish people and their history. Rather, from the particularistic perspective of the Jewish people with their particular cultural inheritance of texts called "Rabbinic" and "Jewish," Jewish philosophy attempts to understand as well as it can all of inanimate and animate life in a historical perspective. For the moment let's leave aside the question of what makes this kind of philosophy "Jewish"; let's focus rather on what makes it "philosophy," for with this usage of the term there may today be more academic research and reflection relevant to preserving and/or evolving Jewish faith in schools of the physical sciences (especially in physical cosmology) and the life sciences (especially in evolutionary biology) than there is in contemporary departments of philosophy where the focus of critical attention is increasingly on certain kinds of cognitive use of human language.

THE CHALLENGES OF THE MODERN SCIENCES FOR JEWISH FAITH 83

The challenges to Jewish faith are not limited exclusively to the encounter between Greco-Roman civilization and the philosophy of the Hebrew Scriptures. As Mordecai Kaplan argued almost a century ago,[1] every encounter of the Jewish people with a new challenging culture has produced major "reforms" in what this people both think and do, and these "reconstructions" probably were critical for it to continue to survive. Briefly, the Jewish people will not and cannot survive solely by military, political, social, and/or economic force. It will survive ultimately because now as in the past it confronted challenges, both ethical (with respect to practice) and intellectual (with respect to belief), that it had to meet and ultimately succeeded in meeting. The Jewish people has found human resources, Jewish philosophers if you will, who in a variety of ways have exhibited sufficient creativity as well as intelligence, to respond with moral and intellectual integrity, and those responses have both preserved what was best in previous Jewish philosophy, providing the basis for what would become a new (hopefully improved) Jewish philosophy (or even philosophies) for the following generations. Thus a new culture or even cultures of the Jewish people have continually emerged.

That has been true in the past, but it is not clear that this evolution of Jewish philosophy is happening today. I argue that the lack of development constitutes a very subtle but nonetheless real threat to the continued survival of the Jewish people, or at least the survival of Judaism as the cultural structure through which the Jewish people express their faith.

Why modern Jewry has failed to reform or reconstruct its philosophy in terms of the challenges from modern Western science is an important question that goes beyond what I am trying to do in this paper. It has to do with the evolution of the physical sciences and the humanistic academic disciplines since the nineteenth century to our day, especially within the institution of the modern university. The sciences and the humanities have evolved in increasingly radically different directions within an institution that itself has evolved simultaneously in contradictory directions—both as the sole institution for purely intellectual speculative activity and in its growing dependence with democratization on capitalistic pragmatic activity. The failure to reform or reconstruct Jewish philosophy has to do with decisions by emancipated Western Jews during the nineteenth century to focus their confrontation with the dominant Western culture on issues that belong to the humanities rather than on challenges that emerge from the sciences. Other factors are also relevant to this complex story, but

---

[1] Mordecai M. Kaplan, *Judaism as a Civilization* (New York: Macmillan, 1934).

discussing them goes beyond the topic of this paper. Regardless of the causes, what is clear is that the modern sciences raise serious challenges to continued belief in the traditional and liberal philosophies of Judaism, that contemporary Jewish philosophers are minimally informed of what those challenges are, and consequently that perhaps for the first time in Jewish history committed Jewish thinkers are not succeeding in confronting and dealing with the major challenges of the modern sciences to Jewish faith.

My recently published book *Jewish Faith and Modern Science* addresses this problem.[2] The purpose of the book is not to respond to the challenges, although the second half of the book offers a general strategy for such response. Rather, the primary goal of the book is to call attention to the threat in the hope that raised consciousness in Jewish intellectual circles will lead to a serious encounter of Jewish thinkers with the physical and biological sciences comparable to the rich philosophically informed body of Jewish responses to challenges in modern Western (notably French and German) humanist-directed philosophy in the last quarter of the twentieth century.

B. *The Challenges*

Following the topology proposed by Franz Rosenzweig in his *Star of Redemption*,[3] questions about Jewish faith center at the most general level on three topics—creation, revelation, and redemption. I want here to summarize my perception of the challenges to Rabbinic faith from the modern sciences around these same three topics. All three are statements about divine relations, viz., how God relates to the cosmos at its origin (creation), to the Jewish people in history (Torah, or Mosaic revelation), and to both the cosmos and everything within it with a focus on its end (redemption and the end of days).

---

[2] Norbert M. Samuelson, *Jewish Faith and Modern Science: On the Death and Rebirth of Jewish Philosophy* (Lanham, MD: Rowman and Littlefield, 2009). Henceforth referred to as *Jewish Faith*.

[3] Franz Rosenzweig, *The Star of Redemption*, trans. William Hallo (Richmond, UK: Curzon Press, 1999). Also see a recent English translation by Barbara E. Galli (Madison, WI: University of Wisconsin Press, 2005).

THE CHALLENGES OF THE MODERN SCIENCES FOR JEWISH FAITH   85

Here are the challenges to Judaism that emerge from the sciences:

A. Issues with Creation
1. From the history and archeology of the ancient Near East: Are academic bible scholars better trained than rabbis to (a) say what the Bible means and (b) serve as moral guides for our lives? Are Bible scholars wiser than rabbis?
2. From quantum mechanics: (a) The moral value of individuals is questionable in God's physical universe. (b) The existential value of individuals also is questionable. Both problems significantly undercut the rationale for a liberal Judaism.
3. From astronomy: Since constellations are not real, how does the God of the universe relate to earthbound creatures? From microbiology and microphysics: How does God govern particles?
4. From relativity physics: What is the relation of God to spacetime given that space and time are inseparable?
5. From general physics: What is the soul? Is it a form of energy or is it something spiritual or is it something else?
6. What would a cosmology look like that fits the data of physics and astronomy but assigns reality to morality in the physical universe? Where in the modern conception of the universe is there room for quality and purpose as physically real?
7. Ignorance of physics results in inadequate views of the universe in a number of respects: The universe of humanists and other Jewish philosophers (a) is too small and too shallow (too small from the perspective of the cosmos and too shallow from the perspective of the microcosmos), (b) can make no sense out of the notion of purpose in our purely mechanical/mathematical world view, and (c) cannot account for all changes that occur within our universe.
8. Our universe is too old and human existence is too brief for humanity to provide the reason for the existence of the universe. If we give up this humanist assumption, how can we understand why God created the universe?
9. Especially in light of the principle of inertia, is there a good reason to posit a creator of the universe?
10. Jewish thinking needs to rethink ontological monism and negative theology. For guidance in how to rethink these subjects, models can be adapted from the metaphysics of both Alfred N. Whitehead and Franz Rosenzweig.

B. Issues with Redemption
11. The challenge of standard neo-Darwinism to claim that reality/nature exhibits purpose and design.
12. The need to move beyond the dogma that seeing is believing to a new affirmation of the reality of God.
13. The need to move beyond mind-body dualism to a new monism.
14. The need to move beyond mechanistic science to a philosophy of the soul in terms of grounds for analysis of objective morality and of redemption.
15. The need to move beyond life and death absolutes to redefine humanity in terms of a conception of an asymptotic end of worshiping God.
16. The need to rethink the commitment to preserving human nature and restricting moral responsibility exclusively to human life forms.
17. Understanding halachah more in the modes of Eastern religions as a "way" and less in the modes of Western religions as a "law." Beyond all the confusion of the mostly unintelligible rhetoric of Jewish theologians, this distinction is the bottom-line difference between liberal and traditional Judaism.
18. When and how does life begin and end?
19. What does it mean to be "human"? When do chemical reactions become living things? When do living things become human beings?
20. What role does and should capitalism play in decisions about living and dying?

C. Issues with Revelation
21. Should scholars rewrite Jewish history?
22. Is Judaism "philosophy"?
23. Are the Hebrew Scriptures a "fraud"?
24. Are the Hebrew Scriptures "pious"?
25. Are the Hebrew Scriptures "history"?
26. Are the Hebrew Scriptures "authoritative"?

The most familiar to students of Jewish thought are the issues concerning revelation. Question 21 has been discussed ever since the study of Jewish history emerged in Germany almost two centuries ago as a form of what we call *Wissenschaft*, viz., *Wissenschaft des Judentums*, which here means academic discipline rather than "science" since the modern study of history properly belongs under the academic umbrella of the humanities rather than of the sciences. Question 22, Is Judaism "philosophy"? has already been dealt with above. Finally questions 23–26 all have to do with (particularly) German source-critical approaches to the study of Bible, which properly belong to the disciplines of history and text studies, and both of these, like history, are humanities rather than sciences.

It is not that the issues revolving around revelation are not critical. Quite the contrary. Again no viable commitment to some form of Jewish faith is maintainable that does not deal with these questions.[4] But in at least this case the issues are well known to anyone interested in modern Jewish thought, and there already exists a long list (too long for this paper) of important and relevant efforts by Jewish thinkers (notably by Bible scholars and Jewish theologians) to respond. Instead my attention will be on the first two classifications—creation and redemption—and, since it is too much to discuss all of these points in a single paper, I will here focus only on one. My example will be on Question 9. Especially in light of the principle of inertia, is there a good reason to posit a creator of the universe? I choose it because I think of all the issues raised, its centrality is the least transparent of all the claimed challenges on the list.

C. *An Example: The Scientific Principle of Inertia and the Rabbinic Doctrine of Creation*

I want to make two points. First, demonstrations in classical (i.e., medieval) Jewish philosophy of the central claims that the purported creator of the universe exists, is one, and is incorporeal (henceforth referred for brevity as "God") presupposes a Platonized-Aristotelianized general understanding of physics and astronomy. Second, these cited scientific premises are inconsistent with central claims in modern (by which I mean post-Newtonian) physics and astronomy. The proper conclusions from the demonstration are the following: One, it is not that the classic proofs are logically invalid; it is rather that their claims are not absolutely valid but valid only within certain ways of conceiving reality scientifically. Two, the first conclusion entails that theology presupposes the physical sciences, so that theological claims are always relative to scientific claims. Hence, three, theology or more generally religious belief presupposes coming to terms with the fundamental claims of the physical sciences.

---

[4] See Norbert M. Samuelson, *Revelation and the God of Israel* (Cambridge, UK: Cambridge University Press, 2002). Henceforth referred to as *Revelation*.

In my *Revelation and the God of Israel*, I have a section called "The Philosophy of Religion—Proofs that God Exists."[5] There I have argued for this general thesis. Here I want to offer a more detailed demonstration of only a single, although critical, claim in the general argument put forth in the book. I will look specifically at those scientific claims put forth by Maimonides in the *Guide of the Perplexed* as premises for his demonstrations of God,[6] which conflict with the Newtonian principle of inertia in modern physics. I want to tease out the possible consequences for contemporary Jewish theology in this apparent conflict.

In the introduction to the second part of the *Guide*,[7] Maimonides presents twenty-six premises, some of which clearly conflict with the principle of inertia. These are the following: (17) "Everything that is in motion has of necessity a mover."[8] (18) "Everything that passes from potentiality to actuality has something other than itself that causes it to pass, and this cause is of necessity outside that thing."[9] And finally, (25) "The principles of an individual compound substance are matter and form . . . with regard to this, everything that it is necessary to explain has already been explained. The text of the words of Aristotle is: 'Matter does not move itself.'"[10] Pines cites Aristotle's *Metaphysics* xii.6.1071b29–30 for this reference and comments "The quotation is accurate."

In a word every action by an agent and every state of affairs for a subject requires an explanation, in contrast to the situation in modern physics where no explanation is needed for something to be what or how it is; only to change from being to becoming something else that calls for a cause. Aristotle limits the lack of need for explanation for actually being in some way solely to a kind of being called "necessary." With every other kind of being that is not necessary, there is a need for explanation, because anything that (in Aristotelian language) becomes actual had first to be potential, and as potential required something to cause it to change from being potential to becoming actual. However, in modern Newtonian and post-Newtonian physics the entire conceptual apparatus of potentiality and actuality, including the ontological categories of form and matter, are

---

[5] Samuelson, *Revelation*, 176–207.
[6] Moses Maimonides, *The Guide of the Perplexed*, trans. Shlomo Pines (Chicago: University of Chicago Press, 1963). Henceforth referred to as the *Guide*.
[7] Ibid., 235–41.
[8] Ibid., 237.
[9] Ibid.
[10] Ibid., 239.

rejected. Instead, all being is actual being or no being at all, and the kind of things that actually exist are material and not formal.

Newton's first law in his *The Principia: Mathematical Principles of Natural Philosophy* reads as follows: "Every body perseveres in its state of being at rest or of moving uniformity straight forward, except insofar as it is compelled to change its state by forces impressed."[11] I. Bernard Cohen maintains that this law follows immediately from definitions 3 and 4,[12] which state as follows: (Definition 3): "Inherent force of matter is the power of resisting by which every body, so far as it is able, perseveres in its state either of resting or of moving uniformly straight forward"[13] and (Definition 4): "Impressed force is the action exerted on a body to change its state either of resting or of moving uniformly straight ahead."[14] About his third definition Newton elaborates, saying "Because of the inertia of matter, every body is only with difficulty put out of its state either of resting or of moving,"[15] and further, "For a body perseveres in any new state solely by the force of inertia." Hence, clearly the terms "inherent force" and "impressed force" already contain within their meaning the law of inertia. Translated into modern scientific, more mathematical language, what this principle or "law" expresses is the judgment that "a body in uniform motion remains in uniform motion, and a body at rest remains at rest, unless acted on by a nonzero net force."[16] In other words, whatever is true of the state of a physical thing, be it rest or motion or anything else for that matter, it will persist in that state unless some physical thing else causes it to change.

Given this central change in physics, none of Maimonides' listed proofs (what he calls "speculations") of God work. Maimonides presents four distinct arguments for God, all of which were adopted almost word for word by Thomas Aquinas in his demonstrations of God's existence in his *Summa Theologica*,[17] and all of them explicitly or implicitly rest on our listed three premises (numbers 17, 18, and 25). The first proof, which is an argument for

---

[11] Isaac Newton, *The Principia: Mathematical Principles of Natural Philosophy*, trans. I. Bernard Cohen and Anne Whitman (Berkeley/Los Angeles/London: University of California Press, 1999), 416. Henceforth referred to as *The Principia*.
[12] Ibid., 110.
[13] Ibid., 404.
[14] Ibid., 405.
[15] Ibid., 404.
[16] See Richard Wolfson, and Jay M. Pasachoff, *Physics—With Modern Physics for Scientists and Engineers* (Reading, MA: Addison-Wesley, 1990), 94.
[17] Thomas Aquinas, *Summa Theologica*, English translation by the Fathers of the English Dominican Province (New York: Benziger Brothers, 1948).

God as a first cosmic "mover," explicitly invokes premise 17.[18] The second proof, which is an argument for the causal priority of simplicity over complexity, explicitly names no premises. In contrast, the third proof, which is an argument for the causal priority of necessity over contingency does list premises, namely 19–22,[19] but not the three that concern us. Similarly, the fourth proof, which is an argument for the priority of actuality over potentiality, also lists three premises, namely numbers 23, 24, and 16,[20] but not the three that concern us. Still, even though Maimonides mentioned only one of the three (the seventeenth) by name, and he mentions it only with reference to his first of the four arguments, it is clear from his introduction to this discussion that he intended all three premises to be precisely that, premises, that is, assumptions upon which his four arguments for God depend.[21]

Implicitly, even if not explicitly, an argument can be made that all of Maimonides' arguments in some sense or another presuppose what Maimonides and other Aristotelian philosophers are saying about the nature of explanation that these listed premises assert. Put in nontechnical terms, nothing comes from nothing. Yet, if a set of causes produces effects that are not entailed in the nature of the causes themselves, then the effects can be said to come from nothing. Hence, it does not seem reasonable that something is moving for no reason whatsoever (contrary to premise 17), for otherwise from where does the motion come? Similarly, potentiality is really not in itself anything at all, for what it is depends both on the something actual from which it originates and the something else actual into which it terminates. Hence, any potentiality presupposes something else actual as having at least logical if not causal priority (premise 18). Finally, as Aristotelian physics defines its categories of form and matter, where form is the principle that accounts for what a thing is while matter

---

[18] Maimonides, *Guide*, 243: "Now, when, in the last resort, we have gone back to this sphere, which is in motion, it follows necessarily that it must have a mover, according to what has been set forth before in the seventeenth premise."

[19] Maimonides, *Guide*, 248.

[20] Ibid., 249.

[21] Seeming mistakes of this sort occur throughout the *Guide* on all kinds of subjects. They read as if the author did not carefully proofread what he was writing, which, given Maimonides' daily schedule of activities as a court physician and as a religious-political leader of the Jewish community of Egypt would not be surprising. However, most scholars of the *Guide* find it unreasonable to assume such a degree of lack of precision in Maimonides' writing and prefer to think that these incoherencies in the written text suggest that Maimonides was transmitting secret messages for a targeted elect among his readers. (Personally I find it preferable to accuse Maimonides of imprecision than intentional falsification.)

is the principle that accounts for the temporal-spatial fact that it is, anything that can be materialized must be in some sense informed (premise 25), from nothing can nothing become real, and only some thing can be something.

Yet this Newtonian principle of the new physics overturns past common sense no less radically than the seventeenth century's new cosmology of heliocentrism overturned the geocentrism of the premoderns. In the new physics no explanation is needed for why something is what it is; prima facie all things merely happen to be what they are; the ruling principle of the state of affairs in nature is chance—an implication of modern science that took two centuries of reflection on Newton's revolutionary conception of the physical world to become explicit. Rather, explanation is needed only for a change from any preexisting state to a new state, contrary to the common sense of the pre-Newtonians whose sense dictated the necessary existence, oneness, and incorporeality of their deity.

D. *Conclusion*

Given this explication of the principle of inertia, let's turn to Question 9 listed above. Especially in light of the principle of inertia, is there a good reason to posit a creator of the universe? How should or may contemporary thinkers respond to the implicit challenge entailed by the above listed ninth issue between modern physics and the tradition Jewish theological commitment to belief in the God of Israel as the creator of the cosmos and everything in it? The religious studies scholar Ian Barbour has argued that there are four possible ways that apparent conflicts between the claims of contemporary sciences and contemporary religions can be handled.[22] The four types of relations are: "conflict," "independence," "dialogue," and "integration." John Hedley Brooke has modified Barbour's claim, saying that usually all four of Barbour's ways are not distinct elements but are joined together in any attempted conceptual encounter with these apparent contraries.[23] For example, let us examine the apparent conflict between the truth claims of post-Newtonian physics that origins in themselves are due to chance and require no explanation to be intelligible and the Rabbinic fundamental or "root" principle (*ikar*) that the universe both has and

---

[22] See Ian Barbour, *Religion in an Age of Science* (San Francisco: Harper, 1990).
[23] See John Hedley Brooke, *Science and Religion: Some Historical Perspectives* (Cambridge: Cambridge University Press, 1999).

conceptually requires a creator. Both claims are methodologically independent of each other in the minimal sense that it is solely the business of scientists to determine what they within their disciplines mean by "explanation," as it is solely the business of rabbis to determine what they mean when they say that God is the creator of the universe. Furthermore, this assertion about the proper domains of the sciences and of Rabbinic theology is for Judaism a foundational principle.

However, both claims are made about the same reality, viz., this physical universe, and some dialogue is required by serious thinking Jews (both with each other and within their own thinking) on what a reality looks like about which both claims can be made. It is not sufficient to simply say "science speaks about one kind of universe whereas Judaism speaks about another kind of universe." If Judaism is to be a reasonable faith for committed Jews who choose not to withdraw from physical reality, Rabbinic thought may not divorce itself from the world of the physical any more than the physical world governed by the laws of physics can be treated as indifferent to Rabbinic law and thought. In the end the initial conflict must be resolved through dialogue in an integrated view of total reality, a reality that takes the laws of the physical sciences (or, the Torah) no less seriously than it takes the laws of the Torah (or, the physical sciences).

One possible solution is to conceive of all of reality in the way that Plato did when he wrote the *Timaeus*.[24] There the cosmos is imagined as a smooth spherical surface that reflects objects of light above it. The sphere is physical space; the objects reflected on the sphere are our physical universe; and the points of light reflected are the deities. As used by the medieval Jewish philosophers and mystics, there is only one point of light (viz., the God of Israel), and the rest of reality is simply a reflection of that single point whose plurality and diversity is attributable not to its source but to the peculiar nature of the reflecting surface. Note that on this model the universe may be said to have an origin, but the origin is not subject to time, which means that it does not reflect any kind of claim that is contrary to the physical law of inertia. However, note furthermore that on this model our world (the reflections) are appearances that have no distinctive ontological status in a universe that contains only two realities—space (the mirror) and God (the point of light)—and of the two it is debatable which has positive being (both, either, or neither), for it could be reasonably maintained

---

[24] Francis MacDonald Cornford, *Plato's Cosmology* (London: Routledge and Kegan Paul, 1966). Also see Richard Dacre Archer-Hind, ed., *The Timaeus of Plato* (New York: Arno Press, 1973).

(a) that the mirror is space, and space is where beings are located, but space itself is not a being, or (b) that God is here understood as a point, a point is a circle (in two dimensions) or a globe (in three or more dimensions) whose radius is either zero or functionally zero (i.e., infinitesimal), and a circular object whose radius is zero is itself nothing at all.

Plato's *Timaeus* is not the only way that we may and even have imaged a cosmos in which God functions as an origin independent of any notion of efficient temporal cause. The most commonly used world view today is that of Alfred North Whitehead in his *Process and Reality*.[25] Here all of temporal-spatial reality is imaged as a plurality of "actual entities" that have mental and physical aspects but are in themselves neither. Rather they are more "occasions," that is, events or (in the language of modern logic) "states of affairs" that flow in space through time from one occasion into another. Here reality is imagined somewhat as it appears through a microscope—as a sea of fluid beings constantly flowing past, through, and into each other, ultimately coalescing to form new actual entities. The things in the sea and the sea itself together constitute a living, changing being in which everything else is fluid. This fluidity is conceived in terms of a dynamic flow, a flow that exhibits direction but no starting point or ending point. There is no beginning or end in any finite temporal sense, but the flow is conceived in terms of a nontemporal origin and a nontemporal end. That origin is described as containing the seemingly infinite potential of everything that the actual entities may become throughout the flow of physical and mental reality. Conversely the end is described as what it is that everything will coalesce to become when every potentiality is exhausted and reality reaches the idealized, asymptotic end towards which everything is moving. However this end is ideal and not real (to use the mathematical language of Hermann Cohen). It is an end that directs an infinite flow, but the end itself is finite. It functions eternally as an end or ideal (again in Hermann Cohen's language) that is beyond time. Whitehead calls this infinite repository of an idealized universe at its origin "the primordial nature of God," and the idealized universe at its end "the consequent nature of God." Note that, consistent with the law of inertia, what is real (as opposed to ideal) is the directed motion of transitory beings from an infinitely remote past towards an equally infinitely remote future.

---

[25] Alfred North Whitehead, *Process and Reality: Corrected Edition*, ed. David Ray Griffin and Donald W. Sherburne (New York: The Free Press, 1978).

I have intentionally built into the above description of Whitehead references to the reasoned cosmic picture of Hermann Cohen, even though I have no basis to believe that either philosopher was familiar with the other. I do so to call attention to the similarity between the envisioned cosmos of Whitehead and its counterpart in Cohen's disciple, Franz Rosenzweig.[26] In his *Star of Redemption*, Rosenzweig images the created world of physical objects as an unending flow of potential nothings changing continuously towards a final end of becoming some-things, an end in a "kingdom of God" where every potentiality will be realized and come together as a single light that replaces all darkness in which, in the words of traditional Jewish liturgy, "on that day the Lord will be one and his name will be one." Rosenzweig images this world as a spatial domain filled with darkness where emerging some-things fill, and thereby enlighten, the empty space. Within the space of this world the emergent some-things are animate and inanimate; the animate beings are human and nonhuman, and the human beings are pagans, Christians, and Jews. In Rosenzweig's conception of the divine kingdom at the end of everything (beyond the traditional Rabbinic "end of days") Rosenzweig images the disappearance of everything into a single universal light. Following Maimonides' negative theology, Rosenzweig tells us that God by definition is not anything that is, so that each thing that becomes something defines God by God not being him/her/it. In the end God is fully defined by a fully emerging universe that is not God, but because this plenitude of light is all that is, at this final asymptotic end, there no longer is any distinction between God and the world.

The parallels between Rosenzweig's Cohenian conception of the cosmos and Whitehead's seem to me to be obvious, and the source of the identity is not any shared historical influence, but shared traditions of Western religion and modern science, which, in both cases, are directed towards integrating the biblical religious traditions of textual commentary with seemingly conflicting modern Western scientific claims, the most important of which (for our present purposes) being Newton's first law of motion, the principle of inertia.

What this discussion of the seeming but no more than apparent contradiction between the modern physical principle of inertia and the traditional Rabbinic principle of divine creation illustrates is how a creative religious thinker of the quality of Rosenzweig engaged modern science with

---

[26] I leave for another paper a more complete discussion of the parallels between Whitehead and Rosenzweig.

sophisticated religious faith. Despite the many attempts by contemporary commentators on his writings to the contrary, Rosenzweig was not an anti-rationalist who claimed the truth of Judaism despite reason. On the contrary, while he affirmed that the domain of revealed belief transcends the domain of human scientific and philosophic knowledge, a proper interpretation of the former did not and could not contradict a legitimate application of the latter. Both faith and reason had significant and complementary roles to play in the pursuit of the true, and it is the true that is the goal of both science and religion. The speculative writings of Rosenzweig about Jewish texts and Whitehead about Christian doctrine present prime examples of how Western people of faith can and should struggle to integrate their spiritual life with their humanist pursuit through science of wisdom.

INTERVIEW WITH NORBERT M. SAMUELSON
OCTOBER 17, 2012

Hava Tirosh-Samuelson and Aaron W. Hughes

Professor Samuelson, you are an ordained Reform Rabbi, a Professor of Jewish Philosophy, a constructive theologian, a historian of Jewish philosophy, and a scholar, who has written a lot on Judaism and science. Please reflect on the interplay between those dimensions of your intellectual life. How do you integrate these intellectual activities and how did you develop these interests?

It didn't happen by a plan. It just kind of happened. I started out being really interested in philosophy. And every philosopher I read in college, I followed him for the first year. And it was just the most exciting thing in the world, to have ideas, to deal with ideas. So I was going to go into philosophy. And then I found that in school, because my school was not good, there was nobody to talk to about philosophy. But in my synagogue, which was very good, particularly in my Reform synagogue in the Chicago area, Beth Emet, which was led by Rabbi David Polish, you could talk ideas all the time. So, from very early on in my life there was a wedding between being Jewish and engaging in philosophy, a result of the accident of the bad public schools and a really good Reform synagogue.

Can you say more about the public school and about growing up in Chicago?

There was nothing unique about bad public schools in those years. The neighborhood where I grew up, Rogers Park, was half German-Jewish, half Irish-Catholic. And the Irish-Catholics all went to parochial schools, which means that the school was about 98 percent Jewish. The other two percent were the few Protestants that lived in the neighborhood. The teachers were all Irish-Catholic. We, being post-Depression children, identified with the views of the political left, that is to say, our politics ranged from Franklin Delano Roosevelt on the right to Eugene Debs, whom most of us supported. By contrast, our teachers were all Republicans who voted for Harding and Coolidge. The last Republican president before FDR was Herbert Hoover, but he was too far to the left as far as the teachers were concerned, although he was actually a good guy.

So, we, the students of working-class families, identified with the labor movement and even with revolutionary sensibility. Consequently, we committed ourselves to making our teachers as miserable as we possibly could, which was good training in debating techniques. For example, we would have fights about whether or not we may quote Eugene Debs in the papers we wrote for civics class, and things like that. So, I absolutely hated public school and thought everyone was just dumb, contrary to the Jews I met in my religious school who were smart. My family belonged to Beth Emet, the synagogue of Rabbi David Polish, and all the Jews I met there were smart. Therefore, I extrapolated that Jews are smart, whereas Gentiles are dumb. That entailed that if I am interested in philosophy, the only kind of philosophy to do is Jewish philosophy. Only when I got to college did I discover that there were also smart non-Jews.

And how about not-so-smart, or dumb Jews?

No, I had to go to the Hebrew Union College to find out that there were dumb Jews. So, I got over those biological prejudices fairly quickly. But by then it was too late. My mind was set on Jewish philosophy as the intellectual course of my life. I was totally focused on Judaism and on doing Jewish philosophy. In particular I loved medieval philosophy because in the 1950s there were two forms of dominant philosophy: Pragmatism was still very popular, and analytic philosophy was beginning to become popular. At first, I liked analytic philosophy, but by my junior year of college (1956) the English translation of Sartre's *Being and Nothingness* appeared, so that book consumed me. By comparison to Sartre, pragmatism just seemed empty, and William James had no color to him and no particular quality. His *Varieties of Religious Experience* was just emotionally empty. At first, I was a great believer in analytic philosophy because I believed, as most of us did at the time in philosophy, that Bertrand Russell's *Principia Mathematica* and the tools of modern logic would solve all the problems. Within ten years, I knew it didn't solve any of the problems. But the narrowness was going to be the basis of a growth of dealing with everything. It was really a hopeful period in analytic philosophy. I think anyone who had any intelligence had to find out within ten years of being exposed to analytic philosophy that, given its method, analytic philosophy couldn't deliver what it had promised to deliver. When you reached this awareness, you began to look for other things and other intellectual challenges.

As I was exploring my philosophical options, I wanted to find something that had "meat," namely, I wanted something that had substance. So, what I discovered that had substance was medieval philosophy. I simply adored Maimonides, so in college I found analytically trained philosophers such as Gregory Vlastos and Harold Cherniss, who could take the new tools of analytic philosophy and apply them to classical philosophical texts. They became my role models, and I said to myself, "That's what I want to do. I want to use the analytic tools to make sense, not historical sense, but conceptual sense out of the giants of medieval philosophy." But I had very few cohorts with whom I could carry out this project. I had to do it largely on my own.

After graduating from Northwestern, I decided to go to rabbinic school, rather than to do a Ph.D. at the University of Chicago, where I was accepted. Unfortunately, Hebrew Union College in Cincinnati was mostly an intellectual wasteland for me. The only good thing about that fact was that in my first year I had the time and the energy to devote myself to the study of Hebrew. Indeed, I had to work day and night, because I didn't know any Hebrew. So I went crazy studying Hebrew during my first year in rabbinic school, but by the second year my Hebrew was good enough to study the texts along with other students. By the third year, I had nothing more to learn at the Hebrew Union College and not enough to keep me busy. So I went over to the University of Cincinnati, which at the time had a great Department of English where I studied nineteenth-century English novels. I spent two years on the English novel and any sense that I have of art and aesthetics came from those three years of study at University of Cincinnati.

Why did you decide to go to the rabbinical seminary as opposed to graduate school in a secular university?

Let me go back a bit to explain some of my life's choices. When I was in high school, I was going to be an athlete, and I set my hopes on baseball. I really wanted a baseball contract. Alas, I wasn't going to get a baseball contract. So I enrolled at the Chicago extension of University of Illinois because they had to take me. My grades were not great, I had C grades; but in those days a C was not considered a bad grade.

As a high school student I was a very mediocre student. I would copy my homework from the girl next to me during homeroom, and I did not really put any effort into my studies. But in Hebrew school, that's another story. Whereas in public school I did nothing, in Hebrew school I worked very hard and was very creative. For example, when Chayim Weitzman's biography came out, I turned it into a play, which was produced by my confirmation class, even though it must have been a pretty horrible play. So, all my creative intellectual energy was going on in Sunday school, not in public school. I started to enjoy classes only in college, and then I got straight A's. With this improved performance, I was able to transfer from the University of Illinois at Chicago to Northwestern University, where I really enjoyed myself and became a real student. I was majoring in philosophy and the department at that point was filled with philosophers who were mostly pragmatists. This was a wonderful intellectual experience, and I had a wonderful time studying.

When I graduated from Northwestern, I had to make a decision. And now I return to the question: why did I go to rabbinic seminary as opposed to graduate school? At the time, my cousin, David Weissman, who was also my good friend, and I studied together all the time; we were together all the time, and we both got full scholarships to the Department of Philosophy at the University of Chicago. Professor Richard McKeon, the great scholar of Aristotle, wanted me to come to study with him, and I was faced with a serious decision. Jewish philosophy was very important to me, but there were no prospects for a job in Jewish studies in the late 1950s. There were simply no academic positions in Jewish studies. Given my intellectual interests, the only way to be employed was to become a Hillel director, because in those days, the best people were Hillel directors. Intellectually, the best people were Hillel directors because in that capacity you could teach Jewish studies courses, and you could also study whatever you want. As a rabbi of a congregation, one was rather limited in terms of academic pursuits, but in Hillel there were no limits; you could make the position to be as academic as you want. Some of the best minds in America during those years were Hillel rabbis: Max Ticktin, Richard Israel, Maurice Peckarsky, and others were just terrific. So in the 1950s and 1960s the best intellectual life Jewishly could be found in Hillel Foundations on American campuses. The heyday of Hillel Foundations is long gone, and what undermined them was the opening of Jewish studies programs in American universities, which happened in earnest during the 1970s. Now the best people who wanted to devote their life to the academic study of Judaism went into Jewish studies, and Hillel Foundations just couldn't do it anymore.

Anyway, when I graduated college I had to decide what I wanted to do and I opted for the rabbinic degree first. Now, that says a lot about me as a person. It not only indicated that the Jewish came first and was most important for me, but also that was the existential way of making a decision. Do I go and study with Richard McKeon for probably twenty years, given his impossible demands and expectations, or do I want to go to the Hebrew Union College and become a rabbi first? So, the plan was to go to Hebrew Union College and become a rabbi and then get a job as a rabbi that will enable me to study for the Ph.D. Making a decent living was very important to me; I did not want to starve to death no matter how much I loved philosophy.

Making a living was significant particularly because, being born in 1936, I was a product of the Great Depression. So I was enrolled in Hebrew Union College and by chance Professor Norman Golb came to the Hebrew Union College to teach. As you know, he was a great scholar but he lasted only two years at Hebrew Union College because he did not fit the institution. But for me, the presence of Golb on the faculty was an important turning point. He was wonderful for me and I spent two years studying Arabic with him and working on Ibn Rushd's *Fasl al-Maqal* (The Decisive Treatise). We spent a year reading the text very closely, and he opened up medieval Jewish philosophy for me. Golb introduced me to the works of Harry Austryn Wolfson and I fell in love with his wonderful work *Crescas' Critique of Aristotle: Problems of Aristotle's Physics in Jewish and Arabic Philosophy* (1929) the first time I read it. I said to myself, "I'm going to be just like Harry Wolfson. I'm going to do Jewish philosophy even better than he did, because I have a better analytic mind than Wolfson's."

Let me qualify this a bit. I knew that I couldn't know everything Wolfson knew, but I also knew that I could be better analytically than he was and knew a lot of what he knew, and that would make me better than anybody else. And so I committed myself to the study of medieval Jewish philosophy. But when I graduated from Hebrew Union College I had to face the question: where do I go? At that time Wolfson retired from his years of teaching in Harvard and there was nobody at Harvard that had any appeal to me at all. Since Wolfson was no longer at Harvard, I did not feel attracted to it. Years later I learned how miserable Wolfson really was at Harvard because of the way he was treated by faculty and administration. But at the time I did not have knowledge about it; it was only my instinct that Harvard was not a hospitable atmosphere; it was not a good place for me. Even though I didn't know intellectually why this was the case, emotionally I felt it. In retrospect this was a sound judgment.

Professor Marvin Fox, who was at Ohio State University, wanted me to come and join him, and I thought about that for a while, but then I met Reginald E. Allen, a leading scholar of Pre-Socratic philosophy, who was at the time at Indiana University and later moved to Northwestern. Allen was a student of Vlastos and Cherniss. Because I liked Allen a lot, I made the decision to go to Indiana University where I got a position as a Hillel director, which made it possible for me to simultaneously do a Ph.D. in

Philosophy with Allen. Allen proved to be a wonderful teacher for me and he introduced me to the work of Professor Shlomo Pines of the Hebrew University, the leading scholar of medieval Jewish philosophy. Professor Henry Fischel at Indiana University helped me to get a Fulbright grant to study with Professor Pines at the Hebrew University in 1967. Fischel was himself a wonderful person and a superb classicist who taught Hebrew and rabbinics in the Department of Near Eastern Studies at Indiana University. Fischel was a tremendous help for me and I owe him a great deal.

I spent a wonderful year with Pines in Jerusalem and found him to be very friendly and outgoing. He worked with me every day and we would socialize. For example, on Shabbat he joined me and my family to drive to Ramallah in the West Bank, which you could do at the time. I do not know why Professor Pines was so wonderful to me, but he was. So that year in Jerusalem was a great experience, mainly because I spent time with Pines. When the year was over I did not go back to Indiana University, because I was asked to assume the position of Hillel director in Princeton. I simply couldn't turn down Princeton so I now found myself in Princeton, which also had a superb Philosophy Department. To clarify let me say that I continued to work on the Ph.D. for Indiana University although I was no longer physically present in Bloomington. Under the supervision of Milton Fisk I wrote the dissertation on the problem of knowledge in the philosophy of Gersonides and was awarded the degree in 1970.

In Princeton you were the Hillel director, but were you also part of Jewish studies?

No. In Princeton I did not hold an academic position as Professor of Jewish Studies and the University did not yet have a Jewish studies program.

So when did you get into Jewish studies and why did you make the shift from being a Hillel rabbi to being a Jewish studies professor?

Okay, well, let's take the negative part first and then the positive part. You can only organize so many "Save the Russian Jews" rallies, right? I mean, after a while, if you're going to stay in Hillel and not deteriorate, you go to the national office or do something else. And to go to the national office was to be an administrator. And I had no desire to become part of the national office at Hillel. Also, Hillel was changing. Hillel was not going to be under B'nai B'rith anymore but rather under the local Jewish federations.

And under the auspices of a local Jewish federation, I would not have the freedom to build the kind of a "mini-Samuelson university" I put together as a Hillel director first in Indiana and then in Princeton. I could do that only because I was operating through Hillel. As a Hillel director I could ignore students I didn't want to deal with, but if I were working for a Jewish federation, I had to be accessible for everybody. My intellectual priorities were not the priorities of the federation. So I figured out that Hillel was no longer a good place to be; I had to change course and find another home for my intellectual pursuits. In the mid-1970s thanks to Black studies, programs of Jewish studies were opening up all over the United States and that was to be my new intellectual home.

Jewish studies emerged in the U.S. piggy-backing on Black studies. Let me give you an example from Brooklyn College. I actually introduced Jewish studies to Brooklyn College. The way that happened is Norman Frimer, who was the Hillel director at Brooklyn, had been fighting for a long time to get a Jewish studies position at Brooklyn College. And nobody would do it; particularly, the Jews didn't want it. And it turned out that three people in the Philosophy Department had read stuff I had been publishing. So they said, "We're not for Jewish studies, but if you hired Samuelson, we'll approve the position." So, Norman came and said, "Would you go there for a year while remaining the Hillel director at Princeton University, teach Jewish studies at Brooklyn College, and that will establish the position."

Well, I had been doing part-time teaching at Rutgers as a Chautauqua lecturer. And Rutgers was fine, too. But Brooklyn College fascinated me. First of all, I had never seen Brooklyn. And I knew Brooklyn from movies. And I said to myself, "Gee, to go to the places with the names of these streets was kind of exciting." When I went to Brooklyn it was the first time I saw vending machines with "Milchig" and "Fleishig" options. So, I taught at Brooklyn College for a year, and that was enough. The students were all yeshiva bochers, which on the one hand was fun because they knew Hebrew, and until then I had never had students who knew Hebrew, which was delightful. On the other hand, they were the most uncritical readers I have ever met, and these were philosophy courses. I could have assigned them Locke's *Essays on Democracy* and Hitler's *Mein Kampf*, and they would have shown how they agree with each other, because that was their talent. It was also delightful to have students who knew who Lilith was, but they didn't know that Lilith was not mentioned in the Bible. So I continued teaching Jewish philosophy at Rutgers University and working as a Hillel director at Princeton University, but when I got to the point that I didn't think Hillel would be a good future, I looked for a Jewish studies job. In those days, getting an academic position in Jewish studies was very easy. You could practically name your position.

At this point a good personal friend, Malcolm Diamond, who was a professor of religious thought at Princeton University, helped me secure my first academic position. I did not apply for it; he just got the job for me. So the first job possibility was at the University of Pennsylvania. They were just establishing a Jewish studies appointment and we were at the point of talking about what the job would be about, but it didn't look good. The appointment was supposed to be in the Department of Religious Studies, which had huge conflicts, all of which focused on politics, as is often the case in academia. Also, the position was nontenured, and I was too concerned about taking a nontenured position, even though the university is very good. And then the University of Virginia offered me a position. Although that position too did not come with immediate tenure, they guaranteed tenure within a year. So, since in those days, I was more trusting, I accepted the position, not knowing that in so doing, I had pushed Menachem Kellner out of the job. And I only mention that because Menachem stayed at the University of Virginia as the Hebrew instructor, and by the rules of academia, he should have been my sworn enemy. But Kellner is such a sweet, nice, generous human being, that he not only helped me, he also became a good personal friend despite our political differences. I absolutely adore Menachem and find him to be a delightful human being.

So, in the mid-1970s you became a professor of Jewish studies and from then on your work as a Jewish philosopher took place within the academy.

Yes, but by then, the topics of Jewish studies changed.

Before we get to Jewish studies and the relationship between Jewish studies and Jewish philosophy, tell us who shaped your intellectual identity? Who are the thinkers that exerted the deepest impact on your thought?

There are two men outside of the university, more than anybody, who have shaped the way I think. One is Rabbi David Polish, who would deliver real lengthy, well-crafted sermons every Friday night, for about thirty minutes. I used to love to go to synagogue to hear him talk because it was the only intelligent stuff I ever heard. Another person who exerted deep impact on the way I think was my teacher in seventh and eighth grade, a pharmacist, named Henry Kalam. So they probably shaped me more than anyone else.

What about people who shaped your philosophic thinking or who influenced you as a mature philosopher rather than as a youngster?

In college and undergraduate school there was a pragmatist at Northwestern named Asher Moore, who didn't publish much, but was a great, great teacher. In terms of teaching, rather than scholarship, these three people taught me everything I know and would use in my years as a teacher. Asher Moore was for me a model on how to teach. Intellectually, we need to remember that "influence" is exerted more through books than through contact with people. The first book I fell in love with was Mordecai Kaplan's *Judaism as a Civilization* (1934). I think I was in seventh grade when I read the book, and Kaplan's ideas had a deep impact on me; they were also most revolutionary and original. The next book I loved was Jean Paul Sartre's *Being and Nothingness* (1943), which I devoured when it came out in English. I absorbed the book and drove the girls I dated crazy just talking about the stuff in Sartre's book. At the time I didn't know that Sartre's analysis of being came from Heidegger; I simply thought these were all Sartre's ideas, whom I absolutely adored. Had I known it was Heidegger, I might have liked Heidegger a little more, later on in life, but it took me decades to learn that Sartre was a student of Heidegger and that most of the ideas in *Being and Nothingness* were really Heidegger's ideas.

The third thinker who deeply impacted me was Maimonides. I fell in love with Maimonides when I read him for the first time at the Hebrew Union College as a rabbinical student. While I was studying to become a Reform rabbi, I also discovered Gersonides and I decided that as a logician, as a strict thinker, if you want to deal with medieval Jewish philosophy at its most rigorous, you need to focus on Gersonides, rather than on Maimonides. So I wrote my rabbinic thesis at HUC focusing on Book Three of Gersonides' *Wars of the Lord*, which became the basis for my doctoral dissertation at Indiana University, written under the supervision of Shlomo Pines. My initial introduction to Gersonides and my interest in medieval Jewish philosophy all started at the Hebrew Union College. In graduate school at Indiana University I adored Bertrand Russell and a whole group of people who were tied to analytic philosophy. My models for being an intellectual historian were Harold Cherniss and Gregory Vlastos; they provided the paradigm of how to think about the philosophic and religious past which I could adopt and adapt for doing Jewish philosophy. But note that the ideas that influenced me intellectually all came from reading rather than through individual encounters.

So at HUC you were introduced to Jewish philosophy and in Indiana University you were trained as an analytic philosopher. Would you define yourself as an analytic philosopher? What is the relationship between analytic philosophy and Jewish philosophy in your work?

Analytic philosophy is a tool, whereas Jewish philosophy is a subject matter. So there's not a discipline called "Jewish philosophy," and conversely, analytic philosophy is properly topic-neutral.

Does it mean that any topic can be treated by the methods of analytic philosophy?

Well, what does analytic philosophy mean primarily? It's a training in logic that begins with Bertrand Russell's *Principia Mathematica*. This is the foundational text of the discipline, because it provided the tools for doing analytic philosophy. And there is a belief that those tools are useful for impacting the meaning of the text. And what they're most useful for is finding hidden logical assumptions in a text. That's all analytic philosophy is.

So is learning analytic philosophy like learning grammar? Do the rules of logic operate as the rules of grammar?

Think of it as like learning how to be a spy. To be a spy one has to decipher clues, so analytic philosophy offers the right training, of taking those clues and getting at what's going on logically. Analytic philosophy does not say anything about other levels of the text, only on what's going on logically. And for this purpose, analytic philosophy is a useful tool. I still think all people trained in philosophy should have training in formal logic.

Today, as you well know, analytic philosophy as an academic discipline includes not just formal logic but also metaphysics and epistemology and even ethics.

That's right.

So, what is your view of the field of analytic philosophy and how does it relate to Jewish philosophy?

Now, I don't want to call that field analytic philosophy because I want to reserve the term "analytic philosophy" for thinking in a certain way that comes out of the *Principia Mathematica*.

What you referred to is more appropriately called the English-language tradition of philosophy, or the Anglo-American philosophical tradition. This philosophical tradition should be understood as an outgrowth of a certain direction of thought that can be traced back to eighteenth-century mechanistic philosophy. That is a line of thinking, or an intellectual tradition, that begins with Pierre Gassendi and that develops materialist or mechanistic philosophy. Who are the thinkers that are in this tradition is debatable. Because today, everybody wants to treat Descartes as if he's the prime example or founder of mechanistic philosophy, but I don't think that's historically correct. Some interpreters also try to turn Spinoza into a mechanistic philosopher, but I regard this approach to be mistaken.

Whatever we consider the beginning of this intellectual tradition, it leads to positivism. Fortunately, most good analytic philosophers are not simple-minded, although some famous analytic philosophers in fact are simple-minded. An example of a simple-minded analytic philosopher, in my judgment, is A. J. Ayer, so you can always use Ayer as a fall guy on what's wrong with analytic philosophy. That's easy to do because he's so simplistic, which is analogous to using Richard Dawkins as the representative of "science" in the science of religion debate. It is too easy to criticize Dawkins because he too is very simplistic. An example of a good analytic philosopher is Stephen Toulmin, who is quite complex and always useful; there is always something to learn from Toulmin and other philosophers in that tradition. You could always learn from these sharp people, not because they're trained as analytic philosophers, but because they have sharp minds.

Okay, but keep in mind that Steven Toulmin is not a typical example of an analytic philosopher but rather an intellectual historian who integrates philosophy and history of science, and even literature.

Sure, that's right. Now, I didn't pick Toulmin by accident. I think that he actually gives us an example of how to do Jewish philosophy. Philosophy can be a lot of things and how to define it depends on what you're interested in. I'm reluctant to say, Jewish philosophy is X, Y, and Z, and I don't want to generalize about the task of philosophy. If people want to do grammar as philosophers, they can do grammar as philosophers. Personally, I've always been interested in cosmology. From the beginning of my graduate studies, I've been interested in the picture of the universe, rather than in human beings. I'm not primarily interested in human beings, although I am interested in human beings in terms of how they fit into the order of things. For example, for the past decade, I have been very interested in light and its philosophic and religious significance. Light in the Bible is an entity.

Light in Aristotelian philosophy is real but it's not an entity. You make a list of what exists in the universe according to Aristotle, and you realize that there's no light. I find that interesting that for the ancient Greek philosophers, the universe is without light.

That is because the ancient Greek philosophers identified matter with darkness.

That's right. I mean, it's really kind of interesting. So, I like those kinds of questions and for me philosophy is what enables you to ask those kinds of questions. Now, if I were going to school today, would I get a degree in philosophy? No. Not the way philosophy is taught in this country. If I were going to school today, I would get a degree in astrophysics or cosmology, by which I refer to the science of physical cosmology.

In other words, you would focus on science rather than on philosophy. But wouldn't study of the history of science or philosophy of science be of greater interest to you?

Well, whether I could study science, such as astrophysics, is a question of my abilities. But in general the issues that interest me intellectually are decided today by scientists rather than by philosophers.

So if I were starting over today, I would have become a scientist. Now, I have always had a historic interest, but before doing a degree in the history of science, I would first get a degree in cosmology, and then do history of science. But I think you're absolutely right: in order to understand science, we need a historical perspective. Minimally, it gives you the humility to know that you're not there yet; that wherever you are intellectually, you will be surpassed. That insight has always been enormously comforting, so that's philosophy.

Now let me reflect on Jewish philosophy. First, I've always preferred being Jewish, over any other identity, since from early childhood I regarded Judaism to be intellectually compelling. My whole intellectual life has been studying Jewish texts as part of being a Jew. Second, I have a strong commitment to being Jewish, which is for me a primary commitment. It's like being an Israeli and you choose to take a job in Israel, even though you could go someplace else, because you want to stay in Israel. I always have a preference for being Jewish, which for me is a religious commitment. So the commitment to being Jewish is religiously primary; it's an existential commitment. So, that's why I focus on Jewish philosophy over and above other intellectual pursuits such as history and philosophy of science, cosmology, physics, or astrophysics.

I'll give you another example to illustrate the relationship between Jewish philosophy and philosophy in general. I am trying to write the history of conceptions of light from antiquity to the present, and I got to the seventeenth century. Now it turns out that the Jews, except for some kabbalists, were not so interested in the nature and character of light. Within the history of Western philosophy, the guy who's the most interesting in this regard is Francesco Patrizzi, who taught at the University of Rome. And if I were going to write just a philosophical continuity of the history of the development of light, I would focus on this thinker.

Within Jewish reflections on light, you would have to focus on kabbalistic texts. So far, you have not written about Kabbalah, which had much to say about light.

Yes, because Frances Yates has written on Kabbalah in the context of Renaissance science and it seems to be that she covered the topic.

But Yates did not really know the kabbalistic material on light.

Yes, that's right.

There's a whole tradition that is relevant to your attempt to write the history of Jewish conceptions of light which remains understudied.

Yeah, but isn't it interesting that in the seventeenth century, the person who puts it together is a non-Jew?

How do you respond to the fact that analytical philosophers (and analytic philosophy in general) just aren't interested in Jewish philosophy?

I have much to say about that. First of all, if we think about analytic philosophy broadly as the Anglo-American philosophical tradition, this is actually a sociological question. One reason why this tradition ignores the Jewish aspect arises from the fact that it is a Marxist tradition, and Marx and Marxism have been deeply critical of religion and have no use for Judaism. We don't talk about it when we think about Anglo-American philosophy, but we should. Marxism implies a strong commitment to materialism and secularism, the result of which is the antireligious commitment that characterizes England in the nineteenth and early twentieth centuries. And again, we don't talk about that. But that's where the commitments are political commitments and the rejection of religion is part of the Marxist orientation of the Anglo-American tradition. That's one reason. Paradoxically, there's a deep religious commitment to irreligion. There's a deep religious commitment to materialism.

You mean that in Anglo-American philosophy there is a dogmatic commitment to being secular?

Yes. I also have a sense that in England there's a kind of soft, subtle anti-Jewishness.

Among Jews or non-Jews?

Non-Jews. It's almost impossible to detect, because it's so subtle. When you try to isolate it and talk about it, people think you're crazy, or oversensitive. But I think that being Jewish in England is difficult, largely because it's so unclear what the Jewish issue is.

Do you mean that in England there is a subtle, under the surface, gentlemanly and polite kind of anti-Semitism?

Yes. But I wouldn't call it anti-Semitism. I'd call it anti-Jewishness!

That's a different story from how to explain the fact that those analytic philosophers would have nothing to do with Judaism as a religion or with Jewish philosophy. Indeed, for most analytic philosophers Jewish philosophy is not philosophy at all.

Well, this is so, because by their narrow definition of "philosophy," Jewish philosophy is not philosophy. So long as they get to have the definition of philosophy, they win. I don't care about it being called "philosophy." I don't care about the name, and I'm willing to grant them the word "philosophy." But if we grant them the word "philosophy," let's get rid of the Philosophy Department. We don't need it. What good does it do? It's so small, so trivial, so narrow, focuses on things of so little importance. Who needs it? Keep in mind that in the curriculum of the medieval university there used to be the trivium and the quadrivium, but we don't have that any more in the university.

Yes, but we still have rhetoric, and it actually is thriving nowadays, so the medieval curriculum did not disappear.

Okay, I am willing to concede that rhetoric has made a comeback. But my point is different: You don't have to have philosophy as a distinct academic discipline that has its own department. Philosophy was not given at Sinai.

But, by that logic, one could say that we don't have to have Jewish philosophy in the university. Who cares about Jewish philosophy? That's the flip side of the same argument.

Right.

So why should we have Jewish philosophy in a secular university?

Well, now you've opened up another large topic that requires further exploration. Let me make my point clear: I have no commitment to philosophy as such. I have a total commitment to being able to talk about the kind of things I want to think about. Whether it's called philosophy or not and whether it belongs in the setting of a Philosophy Department that is less crucial. I'm so blessed to be able to get paid a salary to do the things that I like to do; I would do it for free, because that's what I love to do, but isn't it nice you can get paid to do what you love? Since we are fortunate to be paid for doing our hobbies, which academic unit pays for my salary is less important to me. The key is that devoting my life to these intellectual pursuits guarantees the quality of life.

Fair enough.

So, now, am I committed to being Jewish? Absolutely. Am I committed to thinking about these kind of things? Absolutely. Do I have a mind that likes to integrate everything holistically? Yeah, pretty much.

However, such a mind-set is anti-analytical; the analytic approach is not about integration of knowledge, but exactly the opposite.

That's right. But I try to do both; I can be pretty sharp analytically when I want to be, but I also seek the integration of knowledge.

You are the first person to insist that Jewish philosophy should take note of contemporary science and that Jewish philosophers should be trained in the sciences.

Right.

How do you understand the relationship between Jewish philosophy and the field of science and religion? How did you begin to develop your ideas about Judaism and science?

Well, there's actually a historical answer to that question. My first doctoral student was Jacob Staub at Temple University who wrote his dissertation on Gersonides' conception of space, all in connection with the origin of the universe. It's a lovely dissertation. And on Jacob's committee were Rabbi Bertram Korn, who taught at the department, and Paul Van Buren, who was the chair of the Religion Department at Temple University. At the defense of Jacob's dissertation, Bert Korn asked: "How would Gersonides' theory of space hold up in modern science?" And I had no idea. And I said, "Well, I have to start studying that." As a result of this accident, I ended up studying calculus, which I had avoided through high school because I wanted to play sports in high school, and I realized that I actually adore math. So, it was only while I was already teaching at Temple University that I discovered math. As I got deeper into math and took a third calculus course, I said to myself, "I think I can study this." I got a grant to study at the Lutheran School of Theology at the University of Chicago with Phil Heffner, and he introduced me to the field of science and religion. He set it up for me to be studying with physicists at the Fermi Lab in Chicago, and out of that project undertaken during a sabbatical from Temple University, came my book on creation, which links biblical, rabbinic, and medieval reflections on creation with both philosophy and science.

That's how the interest in science was launched, but I needed somebody to help me to be sure I got the physics right. That person turned out to be Don Lichtenberg at Indiana University, who was a really good teacher of physics. He has remained helpful to me ever since, and I will be always indebted to him for introducing me to physics. It was Don Lichtenberg who hooked me on the idea that the right way to talk about religion and the origin of the universe is in relation to science. Today you need to be informed about science in order to talk intelligently about the questions raised by the Jewish tradition.

Now, the historical context of that is quite simple. Until the twentieth century, there's not a clear separation of what's science and what's philosophy; that separation begins seriously only at the end of the nineteenth century. So, you could take what those Jewish philosophers in the Middle Ages are doing and you can call that "philosophy" or you can also call it "Judaism and science." So, I see my own scholarship to be following in the footsteps of premodern philosophy, except that today you don't do Aristotle and Plato, but do modern science, which is still indebted to Plato. In fact, Plato is a link, or the bridge, between ancient philosophy and modern philosophy. This is particularly true of Plato's dialogue, the *Timaeus*, which is most important historically to the development of modern philosophy and modern science, as it is to the medieval philosophy. The *Timaeus* is also most important to medieval Jewish philosophy, as demonstrated by Gersonides.

Identifying the relevant sources of medieval Jewish philosophers is not an easy task. I'm not always sure about the scope of their philosophical knowledge. Was Maimonides a scientist or would Maimonides have been treated by the Arab philosophers or scientists of his day as just doing Jewish philosophy?

It all depends on how we want to use the word "science."

Yes, that's the problem. Clearly "science" in the Middle Ages does not consist of doing experiments. For example, can we consider Avicenna a "scientist"?

Well, he was a practicing physician.

Right, which had a low status; that's like saying he was a high school teacher amongst professional philosophers today.

No, I don't think so.

We can see the dismissive attitude toward practicing physicians in a comment that Al-Farabi made about Al-Kindi, writing him off, by saying "He was a good physician." This comment means that Al-Kindi was a practitioner, rather than a theorist. The point is that in the Middle Ages, a physician did not have the same clout or social prestige as physicians have today.

I think I would argue with that. In the Muslim world physicians were important people. As for the distinction between theoretical and practical knowledge, that also has a history and is not clear cut at least until the eighteenth century. For example, is Pierre Boyle a scientist?

Well, yes.

Keep in mind, though, that Boyle was mainly building machines to do experiments. By the same token we can ask: Was Robert Oppenheimer a scientist?

Definitely.

Well, I would say, he's an administrator who put together an organization to produce specific results: the atomic bomb. He never did original science. In other words, "scientist" is a messy category.

Yes, it is.

One of the characteristics of modern science after the seventeenth century is a move from theory to practice. So part of the whole movement in the eighteenth century, which was called "the new science," as opposed to "old science," was to do practical things. It's not about theory any more. That's what began to characterize the scientists. If so, I think Maimonides easily qualifies as a scientist because he's a physician.

Gersonides definitely qualifies as "scientist." That is true because of his work as an astronomer. But there is an issue today about Gersonides: since everything interesting in Gersonides came really from Ibn Rushd, can we say that Gersonides was a scientist? That's a serious question. As scholarship on Jewish philosophy developed in the second half of the twentieth century, the dependence of Gersonides on Ibn Rushd became very well known, but I have been so far removed from that field that I wouldn't make a judgment on it.

Let us go back to the field of science and religion. What's your view of that field today? What's the strength of the field? Where does the Jewish component fit or not fit and what should be the place of Jews in the conversation about science and religion?

That is a big question. Let me begin with some background, which means stating the obvious. The development of Jewish, Christian, and Muslim philosophy, in the Western Mediterranean world at least, has always had an interaction. The "Abrahamic faiths" have much in common when compared with other traditions. The Abrahamic traditions share history from the very beginning; they have a common history. But the problem of them being so similar is you might make the mistake of thinking they're the same.

Let's take an example. Menachem Kellner, in his book on dogma uses the word "dogma." Now, it's not wrong to translate *ikkar* as dogma because there is enough in common between dogmatics in Christianity and *ikkarim* in Judaism that it's legitimate to use the word for the two things. But they're not the same, and they don't function the same way. They don't mean the same thing.

The issue under consideration is not so much the relationship between the three traditions, but rather the relationship between science and religion. Where is the Jewish presence in the field of science and religion? It seems that so far, at least, very few Jews are engaged in the contemporary discourse on science and religion.

There are two levels to this problem. First, in contrast to Christians, most Jews aren't aware that science is an issue, that is to say, that science poses a challenge to traditional religion. The Christians are aware that it's an issue. Now, there are several reasons why the Jews don't think it's a problem. Jews today think about themselves as liberal so that as such we don't have these problems any more. Many Jews tell themselves that Judaism is a rational religion, unlike Christianity, which is an irrational religion. Another reason for the mistaken perception that science does not pose a challenge to Judaism comes from Moses Mendelssohn who insisted that Judaism is about praxis rather than about dogmas. If Judaism is about praxis, then we don't have to worry about things like theology, which is of profound importance to Christians, since Christian identity rests on belief. But this perception is historically wrong. In my assessment, we, Jews, have the same problem as do the Christians but we just don't know we have a problem: science is no less challenging to Judaism than it is to Christianity.

Second, the sociology of the Jews is most relevant here. In the modern period Judaism is largely a religion of the middle class, not an academic class. The leadership of the Jewish community, at least in America, consists of merchants, namely businessmen and members of the professional classes (e.g., lawyers, doctors, pharmacists, and accountants) who, as a class, have limited patience for questions that have no immediate practical application. To be concerned with the dialogue of science and religion means to be concerned with things that aren't practical. We can see the problem in the patterns of Jewish philanthropy. I know philanthropists who give money for Jewish studies because they want to enhance Jewish ethnicity; they want Jewish students to meet other Jewish students and get married. But in the university we use the funding for lectures and programs that have no practical purpose whatsoever.

So, your point is that for sociological reasons, Jews, at least in the modern world, have cultivated anti-intellectual postures that undermine the ability of Jews to engage in serious intellectual and theological reflection. Right?

Yes. Unless Jews are faced with a practical issue, or with a theoretical issue that has practical application, they do not get involved. There is a third reason that explains why Jews are under-represented in the science and religion discourse. The field has been dominated by Christians who have their own agenda. For about two decades I have been involved in conferences on science and religion, to which Jews were invited but usually there would be thirty people and one Jew, and the Jew would talk about how Judaism agrees with everything that's being said on the liberal side because Jews of different persuasion or sensibilities were not invited. In this situation, the Jews are no more than a nice footnote in a Christian discourse. Indeed, this has not been in vain, since for the past decade or so, the Jews who have participated in the conversation have managed to show to their Christian cohorts that Judaism isn't the same as Christianity; Judaism is different and the relationship between science and Judaism is different than between science and Christianity. So, what do Christians do now? Are they going to rephrase the questions that inform the field of science and religion? No. Instead, the Jews are simply not mentioned at all, and the discourse remains exclusively Christian.

When Jewish scholars are part of the discussion about the history and philosophy of science, they do not write as Jews, but as scholars that contribute to a conversation which is inherently Christian. As an example, one needs only to look at John Brooke's book *Science and Religion*, which is in fact, as Rivkah Feldhai has correctly noted, about science and Christianity. In other words, Christians leave the Jews out of the conversation because the few Jews who have joined the conversation have convinced them about the difference between Judaism and Christianity. As far as they are concerned it is fine to leave the Jewish perspective out.

You argue that Jews are either not interested in science and religion or they are excluded from it. What does that tell us about the place of the Jew in contemporary society and culture, especially in the academy?

I consider the situation to be as much a problem for the Jews qua Jews, as it is for Jews versus Christians. There is a certain vicious cycle here. On the one hand, we accept and take for granted that Jews are different. We don't want to impose on Christians the characteristics of the Jewish religion. As a result, the discourse of religion and science is really about Christianity and science. Whoever engages in this discourse will learn nothing about Judaism. But on the other hand, the Jews are saying, "Is this going to get Jews to be Jews?" Since the answer is negative, there is no point in joining the conversation.

My response to this conundrum is different. I would say that Jews must engage in the discourse on religion and science because in the long run, let's say within two centuries, if Judaism doesn't make sense in terms of the challenges of science, Judaism will not be able to survive. Judaism is about truth and today science is the arbiter of truth and the source of true knowledge about the universe. If Jews remain ignorant of science, Judaism will cease to be true.

As you noted earlier, most Jews in the modern era agree with Mendelssohn that Judaism is "revealed legislation" in the sense that Judaism is a set of practices, customs, habits of mind, and habits of the heart. For example, prayer is a central Jewish religion activity. How would the knowledge of science help a Jew today to pray more meaningfully? In other words, most Jews do not find science to be relevant to their religious life. But you seem to be saying that whatever Jews believe in has been proven by science to be either mistaken, untrue, or nonsensical. For you, is science necessary to anchor Jewish religious belief?

Yes. Well, we know historically that Judaism isn't one thing and that Judaism has always changed and will continue to change. Within Judaism we can find Jews who have been most interested in science, especially medieval philosophers, as well as Jews, and even Jewish scholars, who turn away from science and focus on literature and rhetoric.

As I see it, to reduce Judaism to literature is a mistake not because a focus on literature is bad per se, but because this is not where the threat lies. Rather, the emphasis on literature prevents Jewish thinkers from dealing with the serious challenges that the modern sciences raise. I have discussed this point in detail in my *Jewish Faith and Modern Science: On the Death and Rebirth of Jewish Philosophy* (Rowman and Littlefield, 2009). The threat is not coming from literature, but from the assumption that Judaism is like literature and that as such Judaism has little to do with truth.

You still need to make the case to Jews, why they should care about science qua Jews. Many Jews simply see Judaism and science as separate domains that have little to do with each other. In their life outside the synagogue they are most informed about science, and for the involvement in science they do not need to associate with other Jews. Conversely, in their Jewish life, they do not feel that science is either necessary or relevant.

Sure; this separation of science of Judaism is a common posture, but it trivializes Judaism.

How would you convince the Jewish philanthropists you just mentioned that science is necessary for the survival of Judaism? Why should Jewish philanthropists care about science?

Look, you have focused on one of my great laments of life. I have never been very good at convincing anybody of anything. I am like the Greek prophetess and priestess, Cassandra, who had the gift of divining the future, but whose curse was that no one believed her. That's me. I always seem to identify future trends correctly, but when I state the point people do not share my views. I simply have no skill at convincing anybody of anything.

Your frustration actually raises an important question concerning the relationship between philosophy and literature. Knowing the truth is not enough; one also has to convey the truth in a certain manner in order for the truth to become known. If you're going to convince somebody, you need to use rhetoric, or what you call "literature," since persuasion depends on rhetoric. You are saying that both philosophy and science have to employ rhetorical strategies in order to be socially and culturally effective, otherwise scientific knowledge or philosophical knowledge remain irrelevant for society at large.

I'm good at seeing, identifying, and observing things, which is characteristic of scientists. But I'm not good at convincing other people of what I see, observe, or understand. Someone else can translate what I see and turn it into a workable program.

To some extent this has happened at Arizona State University. You had the vision about Judaism and science, and Elliot Dorff and you created the Judaism, Science, and Medicine Group, which is administered by the Center for Jewish Studies at ASU. The challenge of the group is to bring other Jews to be persuaded that science is relevant to Judaism and that Judaism has something distinctive to contribute to the science and religion discourse.

That's right. The organization contributes to the solution of a real problem that most Jews don't know we have. Jews do not know that they need science and philosophy in order to be sure that Judaism will not become untrue. But the fact that Jews do not know it doesn't mean that we're not right to do what the Judaism, Science, and Medicine Group seeks to accomplish.

Given the primacy of science and its importance for Judaism, what should a person trained in Jewish philosophy know in terms of science? What is the ideal training of the Jewish philosopher?

Well, I can address the questions minimally, maximally, and realistically or practically. A Jewish philosopher must be well-trained in the Jewish tradition; I take the Jewish religious education for granted. In terms of scientific training, much depends on the kind of problems of interest to the Jewish philosopher. If one is going to focus on the human, then one must study either biology or psychology. These two sciences converge in the new field of evolutionary psychology. But if a scholar wishes to focus on the world, rather than on the human, then one must be formally trained in physics and its related sciences.

Now let me qualify and note that in the field of science and religion most participants are not science experts. What we actually read is not pure science but rather the popularization of science by talented science writers. The consequence is we don't fully understand scientific literature because our knowledge comes from popular science or the popularization of the science. This means that we'll always be behind times, scientifically speaking. We'll never be at where science is really created and scientific discoveries are made; at best we will get there and have some clue about it, five to ten years later.

If that's the case, the enterprise of science and religion is even more suspect, as far as most Jews are concerned. Most Jews who go to synagogue want to pray whether or not the worldview presupposed by the prayer is scientifically naïve, simplistic, or wrong. Jews pray because they find prayer to be existentially meaningful and emotionally beneficial.

Yes, that is right. I agree that prayer can make people feel better, but the goal of prayer is not to make people feel better. Religious life must be based on truth and must aspire to know truth; it is not about subjective feeling.

But most people don't hold this view and do not approach religious life as you do.

That's right, and I believe that this is all due to the impact of Mendelssohn on modern Jewish life. I mean, Mendelssohn reflects the change, or shift, from objective truth to subjective feeling.

To the extent that Jews care about truth it is the truth of halakha. That is why more and more Jews go to Orthodox synagogues. There, when the "truth" is spoken about, it is the truth of halakha, not science.

That's right.

One can go to Orthodox synagogue simply because one loves the liturgy. The liturgy does not have to be true to be religiously or existentially meaningful. The truth value of the statement is almost irrelevant to how you experience the prayers. An Orthodox person is no less committed to truth, but truth is not framed in the context of science.

Yes, I am aware that Orthodox thinkers separate the truth of halakha from the truth of science. Halakhic truth constitutes a separate realm that cannot be critiqued historically or be taken apart analytically. Science matters only in terms of the practical application of halakhic truth.

So, here we once more return to the challenge: how can Jews in the beginning of the twenty-first century be convinced that science matters to

Judaism? How could they be led to care about the scientific truth value of Judaism?

I don't think I can answer that question. I pose a different question and try to answer it: what will happen to Judaism if the worldview upon which it is based is fallacious? For nearly fifty years I have articulated the same message: if the worldview through which you understand your activity as a Jew is totally fallacious, then the practice will collapse. Judaism can't survive if it is based on untruth.

Now, the death of Judaism will not occur overnight. Worldviews do not collapse suddenly or even within one's lifetime; rather, this is a slow, cultural, and historically embedded process that takes a long time, whether it is fifty, a hundred, or two hundred years. I don't know how long it will take for Judaism to collapse if it does not engage in science, but I know that it will happen. Jews will cease to believe in a tradition if they determine that the tradition is untrue. In other words, Judaism is doomed.

This message is hard to convey to the general public, and it is not surprising that Jews do not want to hear it and that they do not resonate with it.

Right. In addition to all the reasons I already mentioned, the reluctance to pay attention to the importance of truth in religious life has to do with pragmatism, the dominant philosophical school in America. Pragmatism focuses on function rather than on truth, and that fits the ethos of America, including the Jews in America. The story of America and the ethos of America is pragmatic and practical rather than theoretical, but we pay for it all the time. We pay for it when children go through bar mitzvahs and drop out, and their children are not going to be bar mitzvahed. The children will figure out that there is no point wasting all that money on a meaningless activity, and they will not perpetuate Jewish education and its rites of passage. In future generations, the bar mitzvah will appear as a silly rite of initiation. But what is one being initiated into? And why should one spend all that money going to Hebrew school to become bar mitzvahed at the age of thirteen? Instead, one could save a lot of money by not becoming bar mitzvahed or use the money for other activities.

So, the whole thing is premised on something that doesn't work. The practice of a Judaism that is not true is like the practice of astrology. There are still a lot of people who practice astrology. Astrology hasn't died out, and on the popular level, astrology is thriving. But astrology is a silly activity.

And the establishment of astrology is a silly activity that goes back to the fourteenth century, when astrology was believed to be scientific. But today we know that astrology is not scientific, and therefore we should not care about it or engage in it. If Judaism is like astrology, then who cares about Judaism? We should only care about Judaism because it is true, but to explicate the truth of Judaism we need science and philosophy.

We can apply this generalization to religion in general, and not only to Judaism.

Well, then, who cares about religion? To care about religion, or take it seriously, it has to be true.

Most religious people, including Jews who attend synagogue, cannot tell you what they believe or why they hold certain beliefs.

Absolutely. But you know, most people are not thinking people. My point is this: if you don't have people doing the thinking you'll pay for it; you'll suffer for it. So, my concern for the truth is the concern out of a commitment to Judaism. So let's examine Jewish religious life and practices in terms of their truth value. Now, on a certain level, I do believe those Jewish activities are true. But the question becomes is, why are they true? And there's a lot of flexibility in that regard. Let me explain the point with an analogy to philosophy of science. The people who do philosophy of science believe that doing experiments is useful; it is a good thing to do.

Well, philosophers of science see experiments as necessary conditions to the discovery of scientific truth. That's the key assumption of modern science: truth requires experiment to be verified.

I don't know that philosophers of science actually think it's about truth, but I am willing to concede that this is one answer. If, on the other hand, they're following Niels Bohr, they don't think philosophy of science is about truth. They think the truth is part of mechanics; experiments do not give you truth, but it enables us to do all these technological things. So there's always a question about the meaning of "truth"; it isn't even just a given what you mean by "true." Part of the question is the value of doing the experiment in science, part of that question is answering, "Well, what do you think truth is?"

There are endless problems about the truth of an experiment. And a good philosopher of science knows all the problems on what is a seemingly absurd activity of doing experiments. Prima facie experiments seem contrary to logic. It's a bad argument. If A, then B, not B, therefore, not A. No. This is a bad syllogism or not a syllogism at all. Who knows what an experiment is? Who knows what is the truth value of experiments? But all the people who were involved in science do experiments and they believe that that there's something about experiments that must be true. Why? Because if it's not true, then science is just nonsense! So the truth of experiment is taken as a given in order to perpetuate the assumption that experiments are not nonsense. But the question still remains: why isn't it nonsense? This is an analogy to Judaism today. No one bothers to think about the truth value of Judaism, let alone engage it scientifically; it is simply assumed that Judaism is true, because without that assumption the Jewish way of life will collapse.

As you well know, postmodern philosophy has launched direct attacks on the notion of truth, especially Truth with a capital "T." According to postmodernism and certain variants of post-structuralism, we cannot speak about objective truth; at best we can speak about subjective truth, or lower case "t," since whatever we take to be truth is situated, localized, privatized, and subjectivized. What is your view of the postmodern assault on truth? What is your view of postmodern Jewish thought, since many leading postmodern thinkers were or are Jewish (e.g., Levinas, and to a lesser extent Rosenzweig)?

I'm not all that convinced on the distinction between "postmodern" and "modern." There is no obvious separation between them, and the usefulness of the terms is debatable. So, for me the distinction between the modern and the postmodern collapses, because I assume one is a continuity of the other. The prefix "post" signifies continuity rather than rejection or rebuttal.

To reflect on these terms, however, we need once more to consider history and sociology. When the Jews entered the modern world, whenever this occurred (be it in the French Revolution of 1789 or the completion of the process of Emancipation in 1871), they became aware of a culture not theirs. As Jews entered the modern world they did not simply become aware of a new culture to which they wanted to adjust; Jews actually believed in this new culture, let's call it Western civilization. They knew that to remain relevant, true, and meaningful, Judaism is going to have to come to terms with it, but to do so in confidence. When Jews encountered Western civilization in the modern period they entered the enterprise saying, "Well, we know Judaism is right, but we know Judaism translates into different languages." In this regard, modern Jews did precisely what was done in the ancient world when Jews translated their beliefs into a Hellenistic framework, and Jews in the Middle Ages translated their beliefs into the language of Platonic and Aristotelian conceptual languages.

In the modern period, the same thing took place: Jews realized that they have to translate Judaism into conceptual languages of the French, English, and German intellectuals. They had to think about Judaism in a new way because they were now living in a world of Newton and Darwin, whose languages Jews could not ignore. The question is this: how does the truth of Judaism we're convinced of translate into this language? In principle, this looks precisely what Jews have done in antiquity and the Middle Ages. But this is only superficially the same. In fact, there is a big difference between what Jews had to do in the modern period to face Western civilization, and that has to do with the nature of modern science.

What we call modern science is really an outgrowth of technology. In modern science we don't give syllogisms anymore; we do not adduce arguments in order to demonstrate truth. Instead, we set up concrete tests, and the concrete tests are all individual. They're not generalized. Modern science introduced a new way of thinking that was concrete rather than abstract, which grew out of technology, rather than the humanities.

The relationship between the humanities and technology has radically changed during the twentieth century. In the nineteenth century and the first half of the twentieth century the humanities had intellectual and social prestige; if you had no mind for literature you were sent to a vocational high school which had a lower social status. Vocational education enabled one to run a machine and make a living on the production line, but it has not social prestige. But now, it's reversed. Today, it is the person who is technologically adept who benefits from social prestige and the culture is driven not by intellectuals but by engineers!

With this in mind, I can respond to the question about postmodernism. The people who interpret Judaism along postmodern categories operated within the old paradigm in which the humanities reign supreme. Therefore, they are preoccupied with language and they believe that Judaism is like literature, namely, just another story, or another myth that Jews tell themselves. Here lies the threat to the future of Judaism. The threat isn't coming from reading literature, the threat is coming from saying if the Darwinians are right, and the post-Newtonians are right, what we have in Judaism is just stories; just another myth.

And Levinas is just another just-so story. So, if you're giving me one just-so story, for another just-so story, that isn't what I need. What I need is what I see coming out of biology and out of physics, and from these scientific perspectives, Judaism is like witchcraft in the sense that it is not rooted in anything, any kind of truth.

Well, how do you explain the fact that Levinas has such an enormous influence and popularity among contemporary thinkers? It is true that Levinas is more influential among scholars of comparative literature than philosophy, but in general Levinas has made enormous impact on many pursuits of the humanities.

Remember, we were concerned about Judaism, not about Jewish influence on general culture.

Yes, but Levinas articulates a certain way of being Jewish which makes a lot of sense in the contemporary world. Obviously, his views came out of his own historical experience as a Jewish prisoner during the war, but his ethical views are applicable to all people. And in the Levinasian worldview there is little use for science, and Levinas's commitment to Judaism is very serious and intellectually sophisticated.

Yes. That's right.

Some people think that postmodernism has had deleterious consequences on Jewish life. Do you share this view?

Postmodernism insists on the primacy of language and privileges literary pursuits. If the world was made up of literature majors, then that would be where the threat is. Thankfully, the world, especially the Jewish world that shapes the future of the Jewish People, is not made up of literature majors. Literature is not the source of authority in the Jewish world. How many people read novels anymore?

Actually, one can argue that postmodern emphasis on linguisticality has shaped contemporary life a lot. Today, the novel as an artistic and cultural form is thriving, poetry and poetry readings are thriving, and these literary pursuits are turned into visual imagery through the media, be it film, television, or video games. Postmodern culture is all about narrative and fiction.

Okay.

It is also possible to argue that literature expresses the deepest issues of our society and culture. Literature is not only about entertainment. Literature today can synthesize life into 150 pages, as much as the Greek tragedians did in antiquity. In other words, literature is a very potent form and a lot of serious thinking takes place today in novels.

Okay.

Judaism today faces the following challenge: what does it mean to exist in a multicultural society?

Sure.

Perhaps the response to that challenge is to be found in literary and artistic pursuits rather than in the sciences.

I don't want to be pulled into the direction of negating literature or the arts, because I am a great lover of these pursuits. Let me make it clear: I knew Levinas in person, and I admire Levinas, and I respect Levinas. My attitude toward Levinas goes back to my love of Sartre that I mentioned in the opening of the interview. I still love Sartre and I don't think that's where the threat is.

You seem to be saying that to be a Jewish philosopher means always to respond to some kind of a perceived intellectual threat. This observation is historically true, but the question is whether Jewish philosophy is only a response to a perceived threat.

I'm not an imperialist, and I do not think that there is always but one explanation to any given situation. All I am saying is that the major threat to

Judaism today is to be found in science rather than in literature and that Jewish philosophy should address the challenge of science, if Judaism is to survive.

One of my concerns is that among serious Jewish thinkers there are people who address the challenge of French and German literature, but where are the people who rise to address the threats of Richard Dawkins? Now, I do not think that Dawkins is a serious scientist, but there are scientists that require a serious Jewish response.

Who do you have in mind?

I refer to biologists and physicists whose approach is not antireligious, but for whom religion is trivial; it simply doesn't matter. Here is where the challenge to the future of Judaism lies, whether the scientist is a Jew or a non-Jew. Among scientists who happen to be Jewish this attitude toward "religion" is common because they're not involved enough in Jewish life.

My point is that a thinking, sensitive human being who is involved in science cannot avoid asking questions to which religion is the answer. All scientists, especially if they are Jewish, must raise questions such as: "What am I doing? Does it make any sense? Should I be doing what I am doing? How does this fit into the world?" All thinking people must engage in this type of thinking because it is about the meaning of life. For this reason I am so committed to the dialogue of religion and science and more specifically to Judaism and science.

Your emphasis on thinking or on intellectual life is understandable, but, as we have noted already, most Jews don't define themselves intellectually but in some other way: socially, emotionally, psychologically, or culturally. Human beings are not merely thinking animals; there are many other levels and dimensions for human life other than thinking.

Yes, but establishing that fact is part of thinking about the meaning of being human. When Mordecai Kaplan gave a sociological explanation for Jewish life (and for religious life more broadly), he did so because he was a pragmatist. It's out of a pragmatic philosophy that prevailed in America during the early twentieth century that Kaplan gave a sociological explanation of Judaism.

Let me shift the conversation to consider another factor we have not mentioned so far: theology. To what extent do you consider your work constructive Jewish theology?

I take theology in a very simplistic sense: theology is the study of God. I do not accept that theology is a different discipline from philosophy. For me theology is a subject matter within philosophy, and almost everything I write is about God.

Wouldn't there be a difference writing about God as an analytic philosopher versus as a constructive theologian?

For me, the answer is no. Of course, I am aware of many thinkers who distinguished formally between theology and philosophy. For example, Rosenzweig distinguishes philosophy and theology. In philosophy, the texts—and Rosenzweig always thought in terms of texts—come from the history of Western philosophy, whereas in the case of theology, the texts are Scriptures. Thus, the second part of the *Star of Redemption* is theological rather than philosophical work, because there he writes a commentary on texts from the Hebrew Scriptures, whereas the first part of the *Star* is philosophy, because he comments on texts from the history of Western philosophy. The third part of the *Star* is liturgy, which is yet something else. But I do not accept Rosenzweig's distinction: for me discourse on God is theological regardless of the texts on which it is based.

Another common distinction between theology and philosophy is that philosophy deals with arguments, whereas theology concerns statements of beliefs or dogmas. This classification is common in Christianity and can be traced to Thomas Aquinas, but I do not accept it either. This distinction implies that in religious beliefs you have to take what's said and it's a given, implying that there is no room to critique and change and object to what's being said.

So, is the main role of the Jewish theologian to critique the tradition so as to reconstruct the meaning of what the tradition teaches?

Right.

Maimonides actually made a formal distinction between theology and philosophy, when he criticized the Kalam theologians (the mutakallimun) for knowing their conclusions before they even engaged in argu-

ment. This is a useful way to distinguish between a theologian and a philosopher: the former begins with the conclusion, the latter does not know what the conclusion will be.

This is not theology but apologetics.

Is not Jewish philosophy on some level apologetics especially, if, as you stated earlier, Jewish philosophy has to respond to an external threat?

No. Jewish philosophy as a response to a threat need not be apologetical. Rather, it requires the work of conceptual translation, of rendering one set of ideas into another conceptual language through the act of interpretation and criticism.

You have written a lot about past Jewish thinkers, especially Maimonides, Gersonides, and Rosenzweig. When you engage in the interpretation of these texts are you doing Jewish philosophy, Jewish intellectual history, or constructive theology? What kind of activity is it when you explicate the work of past philosophers?

"Yes," to all three categories. My interpretation of past Jewish philosophers has philosophical, historical, and constructive dimensions. I am not the only person in this regard. Other people engage the philosophic past in the same way. For example, I think that Elliot Wolfson engages the past in that way, except that he, unlike me, brings to his analysis the study of Kabbalah, whereas I, unlike him, consult analytic philosophy. Elliot and I come out of very different traditions of education and therefore the way we engage the Jewish philosophic past differs in style and emphasis. He engages the past through Kabbalah and continental philosophy and I do it through analytic philosophy.

What do you want to accomplish in your philosophic work? What is the intended result?

Minimally the end result that I want to achieve is integration of what I am doing. I want to overcome the isolation and fragmentation into cubbyholes. The desire for integration characterizes contemporary physics: quantum mechanics talks about the very small, and it doesn't agree with the rules of Newtonian physics, which talk about the very large. Contemporary theoretical physics spends a lot of energy to develop a framework that unites those activities into a common activity. Why? One, because we are not schizophrenic and we prefer integration, and two, because we believe that reality is integrated rather than fragmented. That's a belief. I believe that reality has integrity or is integrated.

So, is it fair to say that your activity as a Jewish philosophical theologian or theological philosopher is to create or construct a holistic system within which everything ultimately has to fit in?

No, I did not say that. What contemporary physics teaches is that the same phenomenon can be viewed differently and can be explained by different theories. For example, light can be explained both by wave theory and by particle theory. Do we really need a unified theory of everything? Making conflicting claims coherent is only one way of dealing with apparent incoherence. There are others (for example, adopting some form of perspectivism). In other words, a so-called unified theory of everything is only one way among many of conceptually reconstructing different insights into a coherent way of living and thinking about that living in reality (whatever it is).

Let us move from these theoretical questions to something more mundane, the place of Jewish philosophy in the academy. You've been instrumental in shaping the discourse of Jewish philosophy in America by creating the Academy for Jewish Philosophy, which was founded in 1980. In retrospect, what is your assessment of Jewish philosophy within American academe? How do you assess the changes in the discipline of Jewish philosophy for the past four decades? Was the Academy of Jewish Philosophy a success story, a failure, or a foundation for something better?

It's a mixed bag. When we started the Academy for Jewish Philosophy, there was absolutely no place to publish anything on Jewish philosophy in American academe. No one would be interested in it. There was a brief period of exception when Steven Schwarzschild was the editor of *Judaism*, and that was the only place that you could publish research or reflection about Jewish philosophy.

Gradually things began to change in the American Academy of Religion (AAR) when Jacob Neusner became the head of the Judaica section. He fought for having many sessions of the annual convention of the AAR devoted to Judaism and to Jewish studies. I remember when Neusner said to me: "Norbert, you tell me how many sessions at the AAR you want, and

I will give them to you." That was an amazing thing, because it meant that Jewish philosophy could be presented to non-Jews within a non-Jewish setting. Neusner made all this possible and that began already in the 1970s.

Still, in the 1970s and 1980s there were no places to publish research in Jewish philosophy, except the Jewish Publication Society, but it focused on commentaries rather than philosophy proper. The *CCAR Journal*, the journal for Reform rabbis, was another place where one could publish philosophical articles, but it was not rigorous enough. So when we established the Academy for Jewish Philosophy, we were all looking around for places to publish and for an intellectual forum that would enable us to get together and share ideas. The Academy for Jewish Philosophy was religiously inclusive and appealed to Reform, Orthodox, and Conservative rabbis, the people who actually engaged in thinking about these issues. Initially the academy met every year to cover an important theme in Jewish thought, and all members would write essays. This format facilitated not only interreligious conversation, but also constructive work.

In the context of the Academy of Jewish Philosophy, I as a Reform rabbi could work with Rabbi David Bleich, who is Orthodox, as well as with Rabbi David Silverman, who is Conservative. The original idea was that each year the Academy of Jewish Philosophy would publish an anthology of essays that would collect all the papers into a single book. It never worked. Why? It didn't work for two reasons. One, you couldn't get everybody to write an article every year. And that surprised me. I was thinking everybody would have so much to say, why can't we just go down the membership list, one name after the other, and get a commitment from each member to write a paper per year? But the majority couldn't do it. That was a major disappointment.

Then, apparently, joining the Academy became useful for people's academic careers, especially at the time when programs of Jewish studies were opening up. We did not want the Academy for Jewish Philosophy to become a tool for professional advancement. But the dynamics of academic life was stronger. Hence the Academy for Jewish Philosophy failed from the beginning.

The Academy for Jewish Philosophy didn't change the university. The university thought then and still thinks Jewish studies is a marginal activity that it doesn't need; as long as Jews are going to put money into it, the university does not mind tolerating the existence of Jewish studies. The attempt to integrate Jewish studies into the curriculum of the Western university has not been achieved, even though there were many good examples how to accomplish such integration, for example, Abba Eban's series, *Heritage*.

If Jewish studies is not going to be funded by Jewish philanthropy, will Jewish history be taught in departments of history? I do not think we have convinced academics in America that Jewish studies is indeed necessary for higher education. Generally, higher education in America presumes that one needs to be trained in what is needed and what they were not trained in was not needed. This utilitarian approach to learning is detrimental to Jewish studies and its future.

But now I'll state the positive about the legacy of the Academy for Jewish Philosophy and Jewish studies more generally. The Academy for Jewish Philosophy produced three generations of books and articles that came out of the interaction between members of the Academy. This created the impression of a so-called Renaissance of Jewish Philosophy, even though in reality the group was very small. The belief that Jewish philosophy was indeed a thriving discourse, or a field of inquiry, is itself positive and created its own momentum. In that regard the Academy of Jewish Philosophy has much to do with the future of Jewish philosophy even though I am not at all sanguine about the future of Jewish studies within the university.

How do you see the future of Jewish philosophy as an academic discipline? In some way you already indicated that you see the future lying in the engagement with science, but is there another potential trajectory for the growth of Jewish philosophy?

Yes. The alliance between Jewish philosophy and literary analysis will continue. I think that's a good thing, although I'm not persuaded that French intellectual heritage is that meaningful or needs to be that meaningful for a British or an American audience. Similarly, I think that the linkage between Jewish philosophy and continental philosophy will continue, although it too has problems. For good or for bad, my feeling is that the Anglo-American model is winning out and will prevail over the French-German style of doing philosophy.

Philosophy, including Jewish philosophy, is now taught in comparative literature departments, in English departments, in religious studies departments, and it's quite healthy therein. We have had many students who didn't fall in love with the Anglo-American analytic tradition, but they did fall in love with Maimonides or with Plato. That means that if we teach philosophy in a nonanalytic manner, its future will be quite bright.

Sure. I don't have anything against this statement.

Are you optimistic about the future of Jewish philosophy within the university?

My view of the future of Jewish philosophy depends on my view of the future of the university. I believe in the future of Jewish philosophy because I believe in divine providence.

Do you mean that God will take care of Jewish philosophy or do you simply say it facetiously?

Well, you know, what else can we do about that? I have more belief in the future of Jewish philosophy than I do in the future of the university. I have a lot of skepticism about the future of the university, particularly vis-à-vis the humanities. So my criticism of the continental tradition is that it is responsible for the view that religion, including Judaism, is a trivial activity. From this perspective, there might be reasons that go back to ancestors and ancient habits of mind, but they will gradually die out. Religion might have some sociological value for which reason we may want to perpetuate religious institutions, but certainly it is a luxury and a trivial activity. Religion is trivial because it doesn't deal with truth, to which the scientists and the atheists can say, "Amen." So, the future of Jewish philosophy and of Jewish studies depends on these issues.

Your response offers a good segue to the whole set of questions related to the place of secularism in the contemporary Jewish existence. One of the novel features of modern Jewish existence is the emergence of secular Jews. What is your assessment of Jewish secularism? Is it really a contradiction in terms or is there something fundamentally incoherent in this position of the secular Jew?

My problem is the distinction between the "religious" and the "secular." Ultimately that distinction doesn't make sense, although it is useful as a political move. According to this distinction, the world is divided between the prince and the church; some activities fall into the hands of the church and other things will fall into the hands of the prince. And the things that fall under the prince we'll call "secular," and the things that fall under the church, we'll call "religious." This view characterizes the premodern Protestant world and what the Protestants say makes sense.

You can argue that the separation between "the religious" and "the secular" goes back to the origins of Christianity and was very much in place in the Middle Ages; for example, in the Investiture Controversy and the struggle between Emperors and Popes.

As a political division of institutions, the distinction between "religious" and the "secular" makes sense; conceptually it doesn't make sense, and it doesn't ultimately hold up. I don't and I cannot clearly say what should be "religious" and what should be "secular." I think that distinction collapses.

What follows from the lack of distinction between the religious and the secular, especially for Jews? Does that mean that to be an intelligent human being, let alone a religious Jew, you have to presuppose a religious worldview?

I am saying that the so-called distinction between the religious and the secular is not clear and all the attempts to make it clear are inherently faulty because it's a distinction that is initially political, not conceptual. For example, I am writing now the history of conception of light in Judaism. The Jewish tradition speaks about the light of creation that is taken away because of the fall, but that light will return in the messianic age. What's that light like? Well, with this light, you can see from one end of the universe to the other at all places and all time. That's how God sees; God sees by this light. That's why he can see everything all the time, because the light is everywhere at the same time.

So, what happens with the establishment of the Kingdom of God? This light comes back. Now, note that with this light, the distinctions between God and humanity are to disappear. The Kingdom of God, then, for the Jews is all about the return to this light. This is the true meaning of enlightenment: with this light humans can see as God sees. So the expectation is that in the Kingdom of God the distinction between the human and the divine disappears. In the Kingdom of God, there is no distinction between the secular and the religious. So in this utopian framework, the so-called secular is defined out of the religious framework.

Fair enough, but note the difference: your example pertained to the end of time, to eschatological reality. You can make a strong argument that in the end of time, all those distinctions will collapse. But we don't live in the eschatological end; we live in a pre-eschatological reality.

Unless you think the French Revolution is indeed the end of time, or at least the messianic age, as so many people, including Jews, actually believed. The same can be said about the American Revolution; many people believed that it would usher a new reality. (Some Jews feel the same way about the creation of the modern State of Israel.)

You seem to be saying that Jewish secularism conceptually or theoretically, and not just historically, doesn't make sense.

Right.

If that's the case, what do you say to the majority of Jews in the world today, both in the United States and even in Israel, who are secular? If I understand you correctly, you tell them as follows: "You are not really thinking through what your views truly are, or what follows from your views." Right?

I generally think that anyway. Let me explain why I think that Jewish secularism cannot work. I will start simplistically and then I will complicate the simplicity. Pure secularism is a mechanistic view of the universe as opposed to a spiritualist causal view of the world. The first world is without God whereas the second world is with God. In the secular world causality is materialistic and mechanical, whereas the religious world allows for a different type of causality, be it God or nonmechanical causes.

Now, let's think about Spinoza. Is Spinoza secular? In Spinoza's world, there are only mechanical causes. Why? Because there's no need for teleological causes and because everything is just a manifestation of God. Spinoza is one example of worldview in which the distinction between the "secular" and the "religious" is not either/or. Spinoza is no simple secularist, as some interpreters make him to be, and he should not serve as the patron saint, so to speak, for secular Jews.

There are many interpretations to Spinoza; some have made him into Buddhist, because he believed in one substance, and others made him into a secularist. It is possible to interpret Spinoza in a variety of ways because he's a good philosopher whose ideas are complex and offer a lot of flexibility. In this regard Spinoza is very much unlike Thomas Hobbes and cannot be reduced to Hobbes. But if the interpretation I've given of Messianism is right, then even Hobbes isn't really secular.

So ultimately, you're saying that secularism doesn't really make sense. If taken to its logical conclusion, secularism is a dead end.

It's not a good category.

Judaism today is a house divided, between the secularists and religious believers and among the various religious self-definitions, be they Reform, Conservative, Orthodox, ultra-Orthodox, and so forth. What is your view on plurality of Judaisms, or pluralism in contemporary Judaism? Is it something that you cherish? Is it something that you think needs to be overcome? What is the philosophical take on pluralism in Judaism today?

Well, I'm inherently a pluralist, and I am not in favor of unity. Unity is something you can impose on yourself, but you cannot impose it on society. For example, I belong to three synagogues in town: a Reform synagogue, a Conservative synagogue, and I also go to Chabad. I'm quite comfortable with all three ways of practicing Judaism and all three fulfill different needs for me. Do I think they need to merge? No, they don't need to merge. Now, I do have criticism and preferences. For example, I would like the Conservative synagogue to be more intellectual and focus more on serious speculative thought. I would love to see the Conservative Movement and its rabbis become less pragmatic. Conversely, I would like to see Chabad move out of its twelfth century worldview, and make it at least to the seventeenth century. As for Reform Judaism, I'd be glad to get them out of the nineteenth century, because they are buried in Germany in the nineteenth century with their ideological conceptions, to the extent that they have not given up on ideology and collapsed into the Conservative tendency of becoming nonideological all together.

So for you, in all variants of Judaism today there is a profound lacuna; something is missing in them.

I think so. If we reflect on contemporary Judaism we need to consider other kinds of sociological problems. Rabbis used to be intellectual leaders of the community. They're not that now. First of all, to demand of rabbis that they become intellectuals means they'd have to read more than they have time to read. Most rabbis today are like entertainment directors on a ship. They're managing this, and pulling this, and that is a full-time job. And the only teaching rabbis get to do is to people below the age of thirteen. Well, there has to be a certain amount of mental limitation if the world is made up of people who don't yet have 100 percent of their brains.

This is most evident in sermons, especially in Reform and Conservative synagogues that commonly resort to discussion of baseball and other cultural forms, in order to become accessible.

Keep in mind that many synagogues no longer have a sermon, rabbis simply tell stories.

Regardless of the actual intellectual life of Reform and Conservative synagogues, can you give a philosophical defense of pluralism?

Well, nobody has an exclusive possession of the truth, because we're human. So monotheism itself entails pluralism. When it comes to practicalities, there's lots of different things that appeal to different people. Intellectual flexibility is useful in dealing with communal social life. A healthy institution has flexibility.

Currently, we see a growing hostility between the Orthodox and the non-Orthodox world. What's your take on that?

Now, that's a different question. And I'll tell you why I think it's a different question. There is a rabbinate that has its ancestry going back to the pre-modern world. And that rabbinate is enormously threatened and rightfully threatened, just as monarchy was rightfully threatened. It is not irrational that my monarchy, namely the rabbinate, died a slow and painful political death. People who were advocates of monarchy were fighting to keep a world in which they were still in power. And that was a losing battle. And some accommodated, and some didn't accommodate. And I understand those monarchs in central Europe who tried to resist democratic or republican trends, but they were going to lose. That's the Orthodox rabbinate. So that people put up resistance and hold up lines and say, "We have to keep modernity out. We shall not mix with modernity." These are frightened people. And they're frightened people who in the course of things will lose. So, I don't blame them for their resistance, because they're fighting to preserve their power, their life, and their identity. In the new world of the eighteenth century, the monarchs were dead, out, and gone, as they should be. Similarly, the rabbinate is fighting for its survival, but it too will be dead, out, and gone in the twenty-first century.

Given your prediction about the inevitable demise of the rabbinate, how do you understand the most poignant or serious challenge for Jews today? Is internal fragmentation within the Jewish people the most challenging issue?

Well, I don't think that being together is an end in itself. It's not an inherent good. Sometimes there should be divisions. And in the case of that rabbinate, there should be divisions. The price of unification is not healthy. Again, what's the price of unification? The price of unification is rejecting everything that has happened since the sixteenth century, and that is too high a price to pay. The future has a lot of twists on it. However, we can reasonably predict the following: one, if we don't reconstruct Judaism, as Mordecai Kaplan already understood, it will die out and it should die out, because it will be obsolete. How to protect Judaism from becoming obsolete is the biggest challenge.

Beyond that, there are two other challenges. Throughout their history, in each period, Jews have always had to reconstruct themselves, not just intellectually, but also socially and politically. As the world has changed, Jews have changed and adjusted with it. Now, they went from being an agrarian people to becoming a mercantile people. In the modern period, there were two major changes that we've had to go through to survive: one was the emancipation and the other was nationalism. The response to the threat of the emancipation was the rise of liberal religion, namely Reform Judaism. That was our solution to the intellectual threat. The response to nationalism was Zionism. Both Zionism and liberal Judaism were wise, intelligent experiments in how to adjust to the world. And right now, both experiments are in deep trouble. So I would say that we've had two tracks of dealing with modernity, one the nationalist track, and the other the liberal-thought track, and both are seriously threatened now for all kinds of reasons. And there ought to be people thinking about it, at least thinking about it, rather than accepting it dogmatically.

Interestingly, you have not mentioned the Holocaust and anti-Semitism as a challenge for the survival of the Jews. Do you think that the Holocaust is an important Jewish theological issue that we need to continue to think through, or do you think that this topic has been sorted out by post-Holocaust Jewish theology and now it's time to move on beyond it?

I think the Holocaust is an event of enormous importance for Jewish history. It certainly ranks with the destruction of the Second Temple. Meaning, an event that forces thinking about what you were thinking.

Do you see the Holocaust as an epoch-making event, to use Emil Fackenheim's phrase?

I do not go as far as Fackenheim, because for him the Holocaust is a new event, and a sui generis event. I don't think it's a sui generis event, but only very important. Any event that involves that many people being killed is very important. In this regard the Holocaust is like other genocides. The question is what's the important challenges in the Holocaust? What makes the Holocaust, the Holocaust? And for me, the most important thing is what it says about modern technology. I think the thinker who first wrote about that is Richard Rubinstein, a very smart man, who in 1967 worked out the theological implications of the Holocaust. The significance of the Holocaust lies in that it took what certain people in Europe had always wanted to do to the Jews and brought it closer to happening. Traditional anti-Semitism could be realized because the Nazis had modern, industrial, organizational methods and better technology, combined with the advantages of chemistry. Chemistry is a critical part of the story of the Holocaust. Now, modern technology in the hands of human beings is a threat we have to deal with all the time. That, to me, is the most important thing about the Holocaust. Is it a uniquely Jewish thing? Well, it points to a special relationship of Jews to Europe. Is that new? No, that is not new. I think Darwin changes the stakes. That's why I don't like to use the term "anti-Semitism" to talk about hatred of Jews or anti-Judaism before modern times. Anti-Semitism is distinctly modern because I associate anti-Semitism with Darwinism, and here lies an important difference between premodern hatred of Jews and modern anti-Semitism. You know, as Fackenheim said, prior to the modern period and Darwin's theory of evolution, a Jew at least had the option of giving up being Jewish. Since evolution is a biological process, you can't do anything about being Jewish. Right? In the logic of modern anti-Semites, the only good Jew was a dead Jew. Now, that is new and it has to do with biology. That doesn't make biology a bad thing, but it suggests, as I have argued all along, that the real threats to the Jewish people are technology and science.

The Holocaust is usually presented as the case of radical evil. Is there significant Jewish theorizing of evil or is it something that still needs to be thought through?

Well, there's a lot to say about evil and the philosophers who do Jewish ethics (for example, Elliot Dorff) have done important work. Philosophically the main point is to realize that evil is real. I'll modify it and say, that in this world, evil is real.

Does that mean that from the point of God, what seems to us evil, may not necessarily be evil?

Right.

If so, is evil connected to materiality?

Yes, well, it may be a matter of perspective that relates to the distinction between this world (*haolam hazeh*) and the Kingdom of God (*malkhut shamayyim*). We live in this world and we only have our limited perspective which is rooted in our materiality. But our perspective is neither final nor complete. We still need to think about the Kingdom of God: What happens at the end of the Kingdom of God? What goes on in the end? Well, in the end, there's only light. All the darkness is gone. There's only light. What does that mean? It means if there's only light, there's no distinction of anything from anything. Without dark and without shadows, there's only light. What does that mean? Everything's dead. At the end there is no distinction between good and evil.

So, the interesting parallel to that is that before the creation of the world, there was only darkness and then God makes light. Then we get the world, with the mixture of good and evil, of light and darkness. But in the end, the light takes over, and there's no darkness. Creation and redemption are matches. What happens at both redemption and creation? The world is over. Before the world and after the world, there's no world. Now, that means that there are no Jews, there are no Christians, no males, and no females. All entities and all distinctions disappear. And there's not even God, because God has no distinction. Let me show you how this vision of the end relates to the science and religion dialogue. A scientist, in fact a Jewish scientist, like Steven Weinberg has discussed that point, but according to him the vision that you get from physics is of a nasty world; the world is nasty. Why does Weinberg think it's a nasty world? Well, because he believes in human beings. From this perspective, the world is a hostile place because humanity cannot survive in it. Take one crummy step off of this little crummy planet, and you die; humans cannot survive anywhere else in the universe, except on this planet and this planet as well as the universe is going to end up dead everywhere. Hence, this is a nasty world, according to Weinberg.

Do you have a positive Jewish response to this pessimistic view?

Well, if we go with Isaiah we will find a positive response. Isaiah also believed that in the end everything's dead, but because he does not believe in humanity, the end is not viewed negatively. I do not believe in humanity. Humanity's days are numbered anyway.

That point is the key insight of transhumanism, which envisions the demise of humanity and its replacement by superintelligent machines.

But even without the transhumanism, we can say the following: humans started as little appetizers for dinosaurs. In the beginning we were like little, round things, and we are not going to be the same in the remote future. I mean, the minimum truth for transhumanism is that everything changes, always. But the universe just can't be about human beings, and therefore the demise or obsolescence of human beings is not negative.

Even if you are right, that from the point of view of God the obsolescence of humanity is not a tragedy, human beings cannot think about themselves from the point of view of God, or even from the point of view of the universe. The only perspective available to humans is the human perspective, so why not stay with it?

Well, the answer is "not necessarily." And if the perspective is going to deal with reality, of course, we have a vested interest in humanity, but humanity can't be the ultimate basis of good and bad.

Even though humans are "created in the image of God," according to Judaism? Your attempt to diminish the importance of humans still stands in conflict with the basic insights of Judaism.

Whatever "creation in the image of God" means requires some exposition, but I do not think that it conflicts with my interpretation of the Jewish vision according to which in the end all is dead. My framing of the issue is an attempt to undermine humanism and its overemphasis on the importance of human beings.

Isn't humanism closely tied to secularism, so in order to demolish humanism you also need to demolish secularism?

Well, humanism and secularism have been historically related, but as I said earlier, I think of secularism as something opposed to religion which makes no sense to me. Humanism, I understand what it is to place your primary values in humans. I think religiously we don't place our primary values in human. We place it primarily in the Divine.

Despite the fact that you put so little value on humans, we want to ask you to assess your own contribution to Jewish philosophy, as a discipline, a way of thinking, or a way of being Jewish.

Well, there are many aspects to my contribution, both positive and negative. Looking at my life in retrospect, I haven't done what I thought I could do and would do. So, how important am I? I don't know. I haven't been who I thought I could be. The positive side is I think I wrote some really interesting things, and I think what I wrote is still relevant and important. I wish it was read more than it's read at this point. My major disappointment is the short life that all ideas, including my ideas, have.

I have been engaged in the reinterpretation of the three tenets of Judaism: creation, revelation, and redemption. I already wrote the book on creation and on revelation and now I am engaged in writing on redemption. I would love all three books to exist as a trilogy. So that would be my most important contribution to Jewish philosophy. But I am also very aware of the short time span within which we evaluate things as "important." How long will that last? Harry Wolfson's work, for example, was most important for the discipline of Jewish philosophy. But today how many people know who Harry Wolfson was? Even within the discipline of Jewish philosophy few scholars still refer to Wolfson, which is astounding. So, everything today has a short life and certainly in Jewish thought. The scholars of Jewish philosophy I read today don't know anybody older than people born after 1960!

In other words, there is a loss of historical perspective both on the disciplines and on Jewish existence as a whole.

I lament this loss not because I'm an old guy, but because as a philosopher I deeply value the historical perspective. To do Jewish philosophy well, one cannot be limited to the last four decades, but must command the entire history of Western thought as well as all periods of Jewish history.

The focus on history brings us back to the human perspective, the only one available to us. But when we talk about humans we have to take gender into consideration. To what extent has feminism, feminist theory, or feminist philosophy changed either Judaism or the practice of Jewish philosophy? Do you think that gender issues are philosophically important or is it just a matter of kind of one fad that will eventually disappear?

I don't think that feminism is a fad, and I think that gender is philosophically, socially, and culturally very important. I'm not sure that I can explain how it's important. Let's take a small example that illustrates the point. I recall a lecture given by Professor Arthur Green on Hasidim. It discussed the Hasidic practice of going away on retreats to study and commune with God. At the lecture, Professor Sara Horowitz, who is now at York University in Toronto, asked: "While they were gone on the retreat, what did their wives do? What was this town like during the week when the men were all gone?" These were a totally new kind of terrific questions that could be asked only because of feminism. Without the feminist perspective, you wouldn't even think about these questions. Now, is there a feminist way of thinking? Do women think differently than men, as some feminist philosophers claim? I have doubts about that.

Well, I actually believe that there is, but one needs to read the feminist literature, and that's what most Jewish philosophers do not do or have not done sufficiently.

The book *Women and Gender in Jewish Philosophy* raises feminist questions but it does not prove the scholars who contributed to the volume think like feminists or that there is a distinctive feminist way of thinking. When the contributors to the volume talked about traditional Jewish philosophy, they just spoke as people, not as women or as feminists, right?

The impact of feminist philosophical thinking on Jewish philosophy is indeed quite limited. It is not clear that Jewish philosophers will take that path or that they will continue to explore the feminist possibilities or the potentiality of feminist thinking for the reconstruction of Judaism or Jewish philosophy.

However, if we move from the conceptual level to the social level, feminism has exerted profound impact on contemporary Judaism. Look at all the female rabbis now. Look how the rabbinate has been feminized. But that too has a price: the rabbi is not what the rabbi used to be.

That's correct: the feminization of a given profession usually goes with the loss of status and stature for that profession.

We do not know, though, what causes what: does the feminization of the profession cause a decline in social status, or is it that the low social status facilitates the entry of women into a profession? And that may be a chicken and egg thing. It's not that causation is just one way. There's no question that the move of women into the marketplace has changed society. But today, do we see a decline of women's entry into the marketplace because people got convinced of feminism? I don't know.

During World War II women moved into the market because the men were off in the army and we needed people to work in the factories. And then after the war was over and the men came back, it was hard to get them to be back in the household and find satisfaction from washing dishes again and keeping the houses clean. Women had to enter the professions in order to fulfill themselves. There were also economic factors that were relevant to the entry of women into the marketplace. After WW II we experienced a significant rise in the standard of living; the economy and the society became more competitive and the only way we could maintain the same standard of living was to have the wife go out and get a job.

So feminism thrived because of sociological and economic factors, not because people truly believed in equality between men and women or because they accepted feminist ideology. For whatever reason, the status of women in the world is not what it was. As every institution and Jewish life has changed, the place of women in society has to change as well. As much as I accept these changes, I am not convinced that there is something about the mind of a woman that is essentially different from the mind of a man. I don't see any evidence for it. This is not an ideological question but a question for neuroscience to determine. Are there any characteristics of a female brain that are female?

Yes, actually, some brain scientists have claimed that the female brain is characteristically different from the male brain, especially in regard to transmission of signals between the right and left hemispheres of the brain. But be this as it may, your point brings us to the leitmotif of this conversation, namely, the role of science. You are saying that all the big meaningful questions in life ultimately have to be addressed through science.

If they can be answered by science. There are many meaningful questions that science can't address. And for the meaningful questions that science can't address, we have just-so stories, namely, myths of one sort or another.

Is religion one of those "just-so" stories?

Right, that's right, but just-so stories are not bad; just-so stories are good things. The attempt of the analytic philosophers to say you can't think about anything unless you can think about it scientifically and clearly is just nonsense. But anything that can be thought about scientifically should be thought about scientifically, and there are many things in life that cannot be rendered scientifically, even though they are very important.

So, as much as you recognize the importance of science, you also recognize the limits of science. With this realization we are going to end this very enlightening interview. Thank you very much for participating in the Library of Contemporary Jewish Philosophers and sharing your views on the nature of Jewish philosophy, Jewish history, and contemporary Jewish existence.

This is a lot of fun. Can we do it every week? How often do you get two bright people to sit with you who will listen to each other? Thank you.

SELECT BIBLIOGRAPHY

Books

1. *An Introduction to Modern Jewish Philosophy*. Albany: State University of New York Press, 1989.
2. *The First Seven Days: A Philosophical Commentary on the Creation of Genesis*. Atlanta: University of South Florida, 1992.
3. *Judaism and the Doctrine of Creation*. Cambridge: Cambridge University Press, 1994.
4. *A User's Guide to Franz Rosenzweig's Star of Redemption*. Richmond, England: Curzon Press, 1999.
5. *Revelation and the God of Israel*. Cambridge: Cambridge University Press, 2002.
6. *Jewish Philosophy: An Historical Introduction*. London and New York: Continuum, 2003.
7. *Jewish Faith and Modern Science: On the Death and Rebirth of Jewish Philosophy*. Lanham, MD: Rowman and Littlefield, 2009.

Translations with Commentary

8. *Gersonides on God's Knowledge: Gersonides' The Wars of the Lord, Treatise Three: On God's Knowledge, Book 3*. Toronto: Pontifical Institute of Mediaeval Studies, 1977.
9. *The Exalted Faith of Abraham Ibn Daud*. Cranbury, NJ: Fairleigh Dickinson University Press, 1986.

Edited Books

10. (With David Novak) *Creation and the End of Days*. Lanham, MD: University Press of America, 1986.
11. *Studies in Jewish Philosophy: Collected Essays of the Academy for Jewish Philosophy, 1980–1985*. Lanham, MD: University Press of America, 1987.
12. (With David Novak) *Proceedings of the Academy for Jewish Philosophy*. Lanham, MD: University Press of America, 1990.

13. (With Luc Anckaert and Martin Brasser) *The Legacy of Franz Rosenzweig: Collected Essays*. Louvain Philosophical Studies. Leuven, Belgium: Leuven University Press, 2004.

Book Chapters

14. "The Problem of Future Contingents in Medieval Jewish Philosophy." In *Studies in Medieval Culture VI*, edited by John R. Sommerfeldt and E. Rozanne Elder, 71–82. Kalamazoo, MI: The Medieval Institute, Western Michigan University, 1976.
15. "Causation and Choice in the Philosophy of Ibn Daud." In *The Solomon Goldman Lectures*, vol. 2, edited by Nathaniel Stampfer, 81–90. Chicago: Spertus College of Judaica Press, 1979. Reprinted in *The Divine Helmsman*, edited by James L. Crenshaw and Samuel Sandmel, 223–33. New York: Ktav, 1980.
16. "Ibn Daud and Franz Rosenzweig on Other Religions: A Contrast Between Medieval and Modern Jewish Philosophy." In *Proceedings of the Eighth World Congress of Jewish Studies, Division C: Talmud and Midrash, Philosophy and Mysticism, Hebrew and Yiddish Literature*, 75–80. Jerusalem: World Union of Jewish Studies, 1982.
17. "The Tenth Principle—Omniscience—Gersonides, *Milhamot Ha-Shem*, Third Treatise, Chapters 1, 3–6." In *With Perfect Faith: The Foundations of Jewish Belief*, edited by J. David Bleich, 440–66. New York: Ktav, 1983.
18. "The Tenth Principle—Omniscience—Ibn Daud, *Emunah Ramah*, Part II, Basic Principle 6, Chapter 2." In *With Perfect Faith: The Foundations of Jewish Belief*, edited by J. David Bleich, 419–26. New York: Ktav, 1983.
19. "Halevi and Rosenzweig on Miracles." In *Approaches to Judaism in Medieval Times*, edited by David R. Blumenthal, 157–72. Brown Judaic Studies 54. Chico, CA: Scholars Press, 1984.
20. "Medieval Jewish Philosophy." In *Back to the Sources: Reading the Classic Jewish Texts*, edited by Barry Holtz, 261–303. New York: Simon and Schuster, 1984.
21. "Gottesbeweise: I. Judentum." In *Theologische Realenzyklopädie*, Band XIII, *Lieferung* 5, 708–24. Berlin and New York: Walter de Gruyter, 1985.
22. "Issues for Jewish Philosophy: Jewish Philosophy in the 1980's." In *Studies in Jewish Philosophy: Collected Essays of the Academy for Jewish Philosophy, 1980–1985*, edited by Norbert M. Samuelson, 43–59. Lanham, MD: University Press of America, 1987.
23. "Judaism and History: A Mathematical Model for a Pluralistic Universe." In *Studies in Jewish Philosophy: Collected Essays of the Academy for*

Jewish Philosophy, 1980–1985, edited by Norbert M. Samuelson, 267–87, Lanham, MD: University Press of America, 1987.

24. "Possible and Preferred Relations Between Reason and Revelation as Authority in Judaism: A Reconstruction." In *Studies in Jewish Philosophy: Collected Essays of the Academy for Jewish Philosophy, 1980–1985*, edited by Norbert M. Samuelson, 127–42. Lanham, MD: University Press of America, 1987.

25. "Reflections on the Logic of Interreligious Dialogue." In *Studies in Jewish Philosophy: Collected Essays of the Academy for Jewish Philosophy, 1980–1985*, edited by Norbert M. Samuelson, 235–66. Lanham, MD: University Press of America, 1987. Republished as "The Logic of Interreligious Dialogue" in *Religious Pluralism and Truth: Essays on Cross-Cultural Philosophy of Religion*, edited by Thomas Dean, 133–49. Albany: State University of New York Press, 1995.

26. "The Role of Politics in the Torah According to Maimonides, Spinoza and Buber." In *Community and Culture: Essays in Jewish Studies*, edited by Nahum M. Waldman, 193–208. Philadelphia: Gratz College Seth Press, 1987.

27. "The Concept of 'Nichts' in Rosenzweig's 'Star of Redemption.'" In *Der Philosoph Franz Rosenzweig (1886–1929)*, Band II. Das neue Denken und seine Dimensionen. Edited by Wolfdietrich Schmied-Kowarzik, 643–56. Freiburg: Verlag Karl Alber, 1988.

28. "Survey Courses in Medieval Jewish Thought: The Philosophies of Judaism: Medieval Jewish Thought." In *Medieval Jewish Civilization*, edited by Ivan G. Marcus, 185–98. New York: Markus Wiener, 1988.

29. "Creation in Medieval Philosophical, Rabbinic Commentaries." In *From Ancient Israel to Modern Judaism: Intellect in Quest of Understanding: Essays in Honor of Marvin Fox*, vol. 2, edited by Jacob Neusner, Ernest S. Frerichs, and Nahum M. Sarna, 231–59. Brown Judaic Studies 173. Atlanta: Scholars Press, 1989.

30. "On Theism and Atheism in Western Religious Philosophy." In *Religious Issues and Interreligious Dialogues*, edited by Charles Wei-hsun Fu and Gerhard E. Spiegler, 21–45. New York: Greenwood Press, 1989.

31. "Gersonides' Place in the History of Philosophy." In *The Solomon Goldman Lectures*, vol. 5, edited by Byron L. Sherwin and Michael Carasik, 105–18. Chicago: The Spertus College of Judaica Press, 1990.

32. "An Introduction to a Liberal Jewish Philosophy of Creation: Confronting Issues of Dogma and Hermeneutics." In *Proceedings of the Academy for Jewish Philosophy*, edited by David Novak and Norbert Samuelson, 393–417. Lanham, MD: University Press of America, 1990.

33. "Judaism and God-Talk." In *Proceedings of the Academy for Jewish Philosophy*, edited by David Novak and Norbert Samuelson, 81–102. Lanham, MD: University Press of America, 1990.
34. "Divine Attributes as Moral Ideals in Maimonides' Theology." In *The Thought of Maimonides: Philosophical and Legal Studies*, edited by Ira Robinson, Lawrence Kaplan, and Julien Bauer, 69–76. Studies in the History of Philosophy 17. Lewiston, NY: Edwin Mellon Press, 1991.
35. "Issues for Jewish Philosophy." In *Problems in Contemporary Jewish Theology*, edited by Dan Cohn-Sherbok, 93–108. Lewiston, NY: Edwin Mellon Press, 1991.
36. "The Role of Elements and Matter in Gersonides' Cosmogony." In *Gersonide en son temps*, edited by Gilbert Dahan, 199–233. Louvain-Paris: E. Peeters, 1991.
37. "God: The Present Status of the Discussion." In *Frontiers of Jewish Thought*, edited by Steven T. Katz, 43–59. Jerusalem: B'nai B'rith Books, 1992.
38. "The Concept of Worship in Judaism." In *A People Apart: Chosenness and Ritual in Jewish Philosophical Thought*, edited by Daniel H. Frank, 245–61. Albany: State University of New York Press, 1993.
39. "Is Jewish Philosophy Either Philosophy or Jewish?" In *La storia della filosofia ebraica*, edited by Irene Kajon, 463–85. Biblioteca dell'Archivio di Filosofia. Padova: Cedam, 1993.
40. "Response to Menachem Kellner's 'Chosenness, Not Chauvinism: Maimonides on the Chosen People.'" In *A People Apart: Chosenness and Ritual in Jewish Philosophical Thought*, edited by Daniel H. Frank, 85–89. Albany: State University of New York Press, 1993.
41. "Rosenzweig's Concept of (Jewish) Ethics." In *Joodse Filosofie Tussen Rede En Traditie: Feestbundel ter ere van de tachtigste verjaardag van Prof. dr H. J. Herring*, edited by Reinier Munk, 207–20. Amsterdam: Kok Kampen, 1993.
42. "Rosenzweig's Theology of Christianity and its Dangers." In *Gemeinschaft am Evangelium—Festschrift für Wiard Popkes*, edited by Wiard Popkes, Edwin Brandt, Paul S. Fiddes, and Joachim Molthagen, 227–55. Leipzig, Germany: Evangelische Verlagsanstalt, 1996.
43. "Theodicy in Jewish Philosophy and David Griffin's Process Theology." In *Jewish Theology and Process Thought*, edited by Sandra B. Lubarsky and David Ray Griffin, 127–41. Albany: State University of New York Press, 1996.
44. "Medieval Jewish Aristotelianism: An Introduction." In *History of Jewish Philosophy*, edited by Daniel H. Frank and Oliver Leaman,

228–44. Routledge History of World Philosophies 2. London and New York: Routledge, 1997.
45. "Nachmanides (Moses Ben Nachman Gerondi)—Ramban." In *Dictionary of Biblical Interpretation*, vol. 2, edited by John H. Hayes, 198–99. Nashville: Abingdon Press, 1999.
46. "A Critique of Borowitz's Postmodern Jewish Theology." In *Renewing the Covenant: Eugene B. Borowitz and the Postmodern Renewal of Jewish Theology*, edited by Peter Ochs, 91–107. Albany: State University of New York Press, 2000.
47. "Judaism, History of Science and Religion, Modern Period." In *Encyclopedia of Science and Religion*, vol. 2, 491–96. New York: Macmillan, 2003.
48. "Revenge and Forgiveness in Jewish Virtue Ethics." In *Lesarten des jüdisch-christlichen Dialogues: Festschrift zum 70. Geburtstag von Clemens Thoma*, edited by Silvia Käppeli, 229–44. Pieterlen Switzerland: Peter Lang, 2003.
49. "Science and Spirituality." In *Secular Spirituality: Passionate Journey to a Rational Judaism*, edited by M. Bonnie Cousens, 110–36. Farmington Hills, MI: Milan Press, 2003.
50. "Tracing Rosenzweig's Literary Sources—Psalm 115." In *Rosenzweig als Leser: Kontextuelle Kommentare zum "Stern der Erlösung,"* edited by Martin Brasser, 481–97. Tübingen: Max Niemeyer Verlag, 2004.
51. "Modern Judaism—Theological Issues: Survey." In *Modern Judaism: An Oxford Guide*, edited by Nicholas de Lange and Miri Freud-Kandel, 267–77. Oxford and New York: Oxford University Press, 2005.
52. "Science and Spirituality." In *The Quest for Liberation and Reconciliation: Essays in Honor of J. Deotis Roberts*, edited by Michael Battle, 16–33. Louisville, KY: Westminster John Knox Press, 2005.
53. "Emil Fackenheim: Reflections on the Evolution of His Jewish Thinking." In *Sonderdruck aus Franz Rosenzweigs "neues Denken": Internationaler Kongreß Kassel 2004, Bd. I: Selbstbegrenzendes Denken—in philosophos*, edited by Wolfdietrich Schmied-Kowarzik, 601–9. Freiberg/München: Vrlag Karl Alber, 2006.
54. "Exploring Rosenzweig's Sources—The God of Maimonides." In *Rosenzweig Jahrbuch: Rosenweig heute*, edited by Martin Brasser, 155–65. Freiburg/München: Verlag Karl Alber, 2006.
55. "Judaism and Science." In *The Oxford Handbook of Religion and Science*, edited by Philip Clayton, 41–56. Oxford: Oxford University Press, 2006.
56. "Rosenzweig's Epistemology: A Critique of the Way of Drawing Lines Between Philosophy, Theology, and Liturgy." In *Sonderdruck aus Franz*

Rosenzweigs "neues Denken": Internationaler Kongreß Kassel 2004, Bd. I: Selbstbegrenzendes Denken—in philosophos, edited by Wolfdietrich Schmied-Kowarzik, 90–108. Freiberg/München: Vrlag Karl Alber, 2006.

57. "Maimonides' Intellectual Integrity: A Critical Study of Ralbag's and Leo Strauss' Criticism of Rambam's *Guide of the Perplexed* in the Comparative Light of Rabad's *Exalted Faith*." In *Maimónides y su época*, edited by Carlos del Valle, Santiago Garcia-Jalón, and Juan Pedro Monferrer, 135–54. Toledo, Spain: Sociedad Estatal de Commemoraciones Culturales, 2007.

58. "Why Study the Past? Two Ways to Do Philosophy." In *Der Geschichtsbegriff: eine theologische Erfindung?*, edited by Myriam Bienenstock, 237–51. Würzburg: Echter Verlag, 2007.

59. "Logic and Language: Reasoning and Demonstration." In *The Cambridge History of Jewish Philosophy: From Antiquity through the Seventeenth Century*, edited by Steven Nadler and T. M. Rudavsky, 188–229. Cambridge and New York: Cambridge University Press, 2009.

60. "A Serious Film" (a film critique of *A Serious Man* by E. and J. Coen). In *Modern Jewish Experience in World Cinema*, edited by Lawrence Baron, 294–302. Waltham, MA: Brandeis University Press, 2011.

61. (With Hava-Tirosh Samuelson) "Jewish Perspectives on Transhumanism." In *Building Better Humans? Refocusing the Debate on Transhumanism*, edited by Hava Tirosh-Samuelson and Kenneth L. Mossman, 105–32. Frankfurt am Main: Peter Lang, 2012.

62. "On the Renaissance of Jewish Philosophy in America." In *Jewish Philosophy: Perspectives and Retrospectives*, edited by Raphael Jospe and Dov Schwarz, 104–22. Brighton, MA: Academic Studies Press, 2012.

63. "Redemption." In *The Cambridge History of Jewish Philosophy. Volume 2: The Modern Era*, edited by Martin Kavka, Zachary Braiterman, and David Novak, 427–64. Cambridge: Cambridge University Press, 2012.

64. (With Eugene Clay) "Science and Judaism/Christianity Dialogue on the Authority of Sacred Texts and Leaders." In *Science and the World's Religions. Volume 3: Religions and Controversies*, edited by Patrick McNamara and Wesley J. Wildman, 1–23. Santa Barbara, CA: Praeger, 2012.

Articles

65. "Ethics, Theology and Occam's Razor." *CCAR Journal* (April 1966): 28–40.
66. "On Proving God's Existence." *Judaism* (Winter 1967): 21–36.

67. "A Therapy for Religious Definitions: Guides and Ignosticism in Reform Judaism." *CCAR Journal* (June 1967): 19–27.
68. "On Knowing God: Maimonides, Gersonides and the Philosophy of Religion." *Judaism* (Winter 1969): 64–77.
69. "Quest for Past and Future." *CCAR Journal* (April 1969): 39–47, 96.
70. "Revealed Morality and Modern Thought." *CCAR Journal* (June 1969): 18–30. Reprinted in *Judaism and Ethics*, edited by Daniel Jeremy Silver, 133–50. New York: Ktav, 1970. Reprinted in *Contemporary Jewish Ethics*, edited by Menachem Marc Kellner, 84–99. New York: Sanhedrin Press, 1978.
71. "Philosophic and Religious Authority in the Thought of Maimonides and Gersonides." *CCAR Journal* (October 1969): 31–43.
72. "The Problem of Free Will in Maimonides, Gersonides, and Aquinas." *CCAR Journal* (January 1970): 2–20.
73. "Comments on Maimonides' Concept of Mosaic Prophecy." *CCAR Journal* (January 1971): 9–25.
74. "Saadia and the Logic of Religious Authority." *Judaism* (Fall 1971): 460–66.
75. "Theology Today—The Year in Review." *CCAR Journal* (October 1971): 90–97.
76. "That the God of the Philosophers Is Not the God of Abraham, Isaac and Jacob." *Harvard Theological Review* (January 1972): 1–27.
77. "Gersonides' Account of God's Knowledge of Particulars." *Journal of the History of Philosophy* (October 1972): 399–416.
78. "Richard Swinburne's Concept of Miracle." *CCAR Journal* (Summer 1973): 105–10.
79. "A Response to Paul M. van Buren's 'Christian Theology Today: Status and Prospects.'" *The National Institute for Campus Ministries Journal* 1, no. 2 (Spring 1976): 64–87.
80. "How the American Jewish Community Could Be Democratic: A Political Model." *Interchange* 1, no. 8 (April 1976): 1, 6–7.
81. "The Ethics of Preferring One's Own." *Sh'ma* (January 7, 1977): 41–43.
82. "Ibn Daud's Conception of Prophecy." *Journal of the American Academy of Religion* 45, no. 3 (September 1977): 883–900.
83. "Travels of a Jew in Germany." *Journal of Reform Judaism* (Fall 1979): 63–72.
84. "Can Democracy and Capitalism Be Jewish Values? Mordecai Kaplan's Political Philosophy." *Modern Judaism* (May 1983): 189–215.
85. "Film Treatment of Jewish Identity: A Reply to Samuel Dresner." *Midstream* (June/July 1983): 42–44.

86. "On Reading Rosenzweig's Star." *Sh'ma* 16, no. 316 (September 5, 1986): 122–24.
87. "In Search of a Model for Liberal Religion: Maurice Friedman's Human Way." *Menorah: Bulletin of the Judaic Studies Program of Virginia Commonwealth University* 11 (Fall 1987): 3–5.
88. "The Jewish Entrepreneur—Academic." *Sh'ma* 18, no. 347 (February 5, 1988): 51–53.
89. "Solutions to Theodicy out of the Sources of Judaism." *Religious Education* 84, no. 1 (Winter 1989): 55–67.
90. "Intermarriage in American Films." *The Cresset* 53, no. 2 (December 1989): 28–29.
91. "Parshat Shemini: Eating as Cosmic." *The Jewish Advocate* (April 19, 1990): 8.
92. "Free Will and Determinism at the Movies." *The Cresset* 53, no. 9 (October 1990): 23–26.
93. "Maimonides' Doctrine of Creation." *Harvard Theological Review* 84, no. 3 (1991) 249–71.
94. "An Appeal for One Palestinian." *Sh'ma* 21, no. 412 (April 19, 1991): 93–94.
95. "The Right to Believe in Jewish Philosophy." *Jewish Political Studies Review* 3, nos. 3–4 (Fall 1991): 59–74.
96. "The Jewish Philosophy of Steven Schwarzschild." *Modern Judaism* 12, no. 2 (May 1992): 185–201.
97. "Science, Religion, and a Medieval Philosopher." *Kerem* (Winter 1992–1993): 65–74.
98. "Tradition from a Jewish Perspective." *Toronto Journal of Theology* 9, no. 1 (1993): 27–50.
99. "A Critique of Borowitz's Postmodern Jewish Theology." *Zygon* 28, no. 2 (June 1993): 267–82.
100. "Shabbat in Hamburg." *Kerem* (Spring 1995): 71–79.
101. "A Case Study in Jewish Ethics—Three Jewish Strategies for Solving Theodicy." *Journal of Jewish Thought and Philosophy* 5 (1996): 177–90.
102. "Three Comparative Maps of the Human." *Zygon* 31, no. 4 (December 1996): 695–710.
103. "Chance and Destiny: A Philosophical Commentary on 'Aaron Should Cast Lots . . .' (Lev. 16:8)." *CCAR Journal* (Fall 1997): 44–54.
104. "Rosenzweig's Philosophy of Buddhism." *Journal of Indo-Judaic Studies* 1, no. 1 (April 1998): 7–12.
105. "Science and Religion: Challenges and Possibilities for Western Monotheism." *Science and Religion* (Winter 1998–1999): 42–44.

106. "On the Symbiosis of Science and Religion: A Jewish Perspective." *Zygon* 35, no. 1 (March 2000): 83–97.
107. "Rethinking Ethics in the Light of Jewish Thought and the Life Sciences." *Journal of Religious Ethics* 29, no. 9 (Summer 2001): 209–33.
108. "Spinoza's God in its Jewish Context." *Prajna Vihara: The Journal of Philosophy and Religion* 2, no. 2 (July–December 2001): 43–72.
109. "Creation and the Symbiosis of Science and Judaism." *B'or Ha'Torah 13E: Proceedings of the Third Miami International Conference on Torah and Science—Part Two: Physics and Math, Humanities* 13 (2002): 63–68.
110. "Creation and the Symbiosis of Science and Judaism." *Zygon* 37, no. 1 (March 2002): 137–42.
111. "The Death and Revival of Jewish Philosophy." *Journal of the American Academy of Religion* 70, no. 1 (March 2002): 117–34.
112. "Maimonidean Scholarship at the End of the Century." *The Journal of the Association of Jewish Studies Review* 26, no. 1 (April 2002): 93–107.
113. "Ethics of Globalization and the AIDS Crisis from a Jewish Perspective." *Zygon* 38, no. 1 (March 2003): 125–39.
114. "Underrated 20th Century Jewish Thinkers: A Forum—Hermann Cohen." *Conservative Judaism* 55, no. 4 (Summer 2003): 56–57.
115. "Culture and History: Essential Partners in the Conversation between Religion and Science." *Zygon* 40, no. 2 (June 2005): 335–50.
116. "Science and Intelligent Design." *The Global Spiral* 4 (e-publication of the Metanexus Institute) (Spring 2006). http://www.metanexus.net/magazine/tabid/68/id/10552/Default.aspx.
117. "Whitehead, Rosenzweig, and the Agenda for Future Jewish Thought: A Response Essay to Bradley Shavit Artson's *Ba-derekh*: On the Way—A Presentation of Process Theology." *Conservative Judaism* 62, nos. 1–2 (Fall–Winter 2010–2011): 152–62.
118. "Reflections on the Distinctness of Judaism and the Sciences." *Zygon* 46, no. 2 (June 2011): 396–413.
119. "The Challenges of the Modern Sciences for Jewish Faith." *CCAR Journal* (Winter 2012): 12–27.
120. "Theology in Judaism." In *Encyclopedia of Sciences and Religions*, vol. 4, edited by Anne Runehov and Lluis Oviedo, 2049–51. Dordrecht, Heidelberg, New York, London: Springer, 2013.

www.ingramcontent.com/pod-product-compliance
Lightning Source LLC
Chambersburg PA
CBHW061840300426
44115CB00013B/2453